MW00641806

# Colorado's
## *Strangest*

*A Legacy of Bizarre Events
and Eccentric People*

Kenneth Jessen

J. V. Publications L.L.C.
Loveland, Colorado

*Colorado's Strangest: A Legacy of Bizarre Events and Eccentric People*

Cataloging
Jessen, Kenneth Christian
    Colorado's Strangest
    Bibliography: p.
    Includes index.
    1. Colorado — History Miscellanea. I. Title.

ISBN 978-1-928656-04-3 (pbk.)

Published by J.V. Publications, LLC
Loveland, Colorado

Edited by Susan Hoskinson
Cover design by LaVonne Ewing
Interior book design by Becky S. Asmussen

# Dedication

Thomas J. Noel, "Dr. Colorado", educator, author, columnist, historian, tour guide and lecturer.

Wayne Sundberg and Joan Day, good friends and fellow historians.

# Acknowledgments

The original idea for a collection of unusual stories came from Lee Gregory, with the encouragement of Philip Panum at Denver Public Library's Western History Department. The best stories from *Eccentric Colorado* and *Bizarre Colorado* are combined in this book along with additional material and illustrations.

Kenneth Jessen
Loveland, Colorado 2005

# Table of Contents

Introduction ..................... v

La Caverna del Oro ............... 1

The Deadly Rat Game ............. 7

Cousin Jacks .................... 10

Indian Eater Big Phil ............. 17

The Pickled Skull Mystery ....... 21

The Billiards Game .............. 25

Captain Sam Heads to the Pacific ... 27

Gold Bricks for Sale ............. 33

Colorado's Diamond Field ........ 37

Colorado's Famous Cannibal ...... 45

Prevaricator of Pikes Peak ........ 56

A Cure for Tallow Mouth ......... 65

The Solid Muldoon .............. 67

Underground Fantasies ........... 77

Bosco's Baggage ................. 84

The Great Rock Wall ............. 87

Pigg Hunts Bear ................. 91

The Hermit of Pat's Hole ........ 101

Legends of the Great Sand Dunes .. 104

Soapy Smith .................... 113

Trackless Train ................. 119

Miner's Companion Is His Violin ... 121

Lord Ogilvy .................... 125

The Hanging Flume ............ 131

Denver's City Hall War .......... 135

Doomed Monsters .............. 140

Leadville's Ice Palace ............ 146

The Healer ..................... 153

Central City's Submarine ........ 157

Colorado's Lightning Lab ........ 161

Quickstep Regains His Job ....... 165

Highest Fort in the United States .. 168

Those Magnificent Flying Machines .173

Three Governors in One Day ..... 176

The Great Horse Race ........... 181

His Head at His Side ............ 189

Colorado's Apeman ............. 193

A Burro Named Prunes .......... 198

Japan Bombs a Colorado Farm .... 203

Elijah, the Marooned Horse ...... 206

Curtain Closes the Gap .......... 211

The Tomato Wars ............... 215

Epilogue ....................... 222

About the Author ............... 233

Bibliography (References are provided at the end of each story.)

Index .......................... 235

# Introduction

Colorado's Strangest combines selected accounts from *Eccentric Colorado* and *Bizarre Colorado* into one fun book of short stories. Although some of the stories are quite serious in nature, this book is designed to entertain the reader with tales about some of the state's extraordinary people and events.

During Colorado's early years, the state's economy was based primarily on the extraction of precious metals. Colorado also developed an agricultural industry. In time, the state's economy diversified into other industries, including oil, transportation and electronics. The key ingredient in Colorado's success was, and still is, its imaginative people. To develop the state's resources (both industrial and recreational) required experimentation that resulted in both triumph and failure. Sometimes, however, the people involved attempted deeds beyond the norm. These activities covering more than a century produced an interesting, fertile, history for those who seek the bizarre and unusual.

The reader is encouraged to refer to the references listed at the end of each story for additional sources of information.

Kenneth Jessen, Loveland, Colorado 2005

Members of a 1932 expedition into La Caverna del Oro wait at the top of the second pit. Note the wooden framework said to have been used by the Spaniards to hoist gold ore. (Denver Public Library, Western History Department)

# La Caverna del Oro

High in the Sangre de Cristo Mountains above the Wet Mountain Valley is La Caverna del Oro (The Cavern of Gold), also known as Spanish Cave. The cave entrance is above timberline at 11,500 feet on the side of a ravine on Marble Mountain. (The 13,266-foot peak is located southeast of the Crestone Peak/Crestone Needle group.) The entrance is usually blocked by a large snowdrift that does not melt until August. Snow often comes to the Sangre de Cristos in September, leaving the cave accessible for only a month or less. A strong wind blows through its subterranean passageways, and its floors are covered with ice and mud. The walls weep with water. This is not a pleasant cave to explore since it consists of a series of steep tunnels and vertical shafts or pits. Much equipment and endurance is required to penetrate La Caverna del Oro.

Stories of this cave began before the Spaniards arrived on the North American continent. As passed from generation to generation, legends tell of gold in the cave. Indians discovered the gold and used it as offerings to their gods. Eventually, the gods became angry, and mining in the cave was abandoned. Spanish monks recorded this legend.

La Caverna del Oro was not mentioned again until 1541. Seeking a mythical city, three monks journeyed north from Mexico. After the death of two monks, the remaining friar found the cave with the help of the Indians. He promised to share its riches with them. Once the monk and his fellow Spaniards arrived, the Indians were tortured and forced into slavery. Much gold was brought to the surface from the depths of the cavern. After loading the gold on pack animals, the Spaniards reportedly massacred the Indians.

Another version of this story tells that the Indians revolted against the Spaniards. The Spaniards were forced to construct a fort in front of the lower cave entrance for protection. By using ladders within the cave's passageways, the Spaniards climbed to the upper entrance and surprised the Indians from behind. The Indians were killed, and the gold was taken to Mexico.

La Caverna del Oro remained hidden until 1811, when a Spanish-American named Baca stumbled across a pile of riches nuggets and gold bars high in the Sangre de Cristo Mountains. He searched for the source of the metallic but could find no trace of a mine.

In 1869, Elisha P. Horn explored Marble Mountain and rediscovered the cave. He supposedly found a skeleton near the cave's entrance clad in Spanish armor. An arrow had pierced the armor, apparently killing its occupant.

The cave remained in obscurity until 1880. J. H. Yeoman located the cave once again and described an ancient fortress at the mouth of a smaller cave a few hundred yards below the entrance to La Caverna del Oro. The walls of the fort were constructed of rock and timbers. Rifle pits surrounded the breastwork. The Spanish legend seemed to have some truth to it.

The cave came back into focus in 1920, when a forest ranger, Paul Gilbert, learned of it from Apollina Apodaca, a descendant of the first Spanish explorers in the area. Mrs. Apodaca recited the legend of La Caverna del Oro. Her version included the revolt by the Indians after being enslaved by the Spaniards. She also told how people would visit the cave and throw blankets into the entrance. The perpetual wind coming out of the cave would carry the blankets back to their owners. She also added that at a depth of 90 feet, the Spaniards dug a tunnel back into the mountain to reach the gold.

Gilbert and several other rangers located and entered the legendary cave. They were unable to go beyond the top of the first pit because they lacked sufficient rope. They did find a dull red Maltese cross painted on a rock near the cave's entrance.

They also confirmed that a cold wind came from the cave.

The legend of La Caverna del Oro moved further away from fantasy and more toward reality in 1929. An expedition was financed by Frederick G. Bonfils, co-founder and publisher of the *Denver Post*. He wanted to see if the legends were based on fact. The expedition consisted of two men, and after they explored the cave, a report was published.

The men reported that the cave's steep passageways were either covered with water, ice or mud. The intense cold and ceaseless wind nearly froze their wet gloves. At the brink of a deep pit, an ancient log was wedged between the walls. An iron chain ladder was fastened to the log. The chain was very old and nearly rusted through. The walls of the cavern were composed of deep red marble with streaks of gray. The men lacked enough rope to fully explore the cave and were able to only cover a small percentage of its passages. No evidence was found of gold or of mining activity.

In 1932, another attempt was made to explore the cave. This time, the party took a lot more rope. Deep inside Marble Mountain, after descending quite a distance, a lantern was lowered on a rope into a deep pit. At the bottom was a skeleton with a metal strap around its neck. It appeared that some poor individual had been chained by the neck to the wall of the cave and left to die.

News of the exploration was published in the *Rocky Mountain News*, and it generated so much interest that a second group visited La Caverna del Oro the following weekend. This group of seven men included some of Colorado's best trained spelunkers. They solved some of the mysteries but added new ones. During the week between visits to the cave, someone attempted to dynamite the entrance shut. It is possible that this was done to keep people out for fear the legendary gold would be found. Numerous Indian arrowheads were found at the fort built below the cave's entrance. This supported the theory that the Indians revolted and attacked the Spaniards.

The party of seven descended the first drop, estimated to be a full 250 feet (later surveyed at 175 feet). At the bottom of this pit, primitive ladders made of tree trunks inset with pegs were found. No nails were used in their construction.

After traveling deeper into the mountain through steep, icy passageways, the party came to another pit. Over the top of this shaft, a wooden structure was built that could have been used to hoist ore. Members of the party could not see the bottom of this pit, even after tossing a flare into the hole. Using a rope, its depth was established at 110 feet. LeRoy Hafen, curator of the Colorado Historical Society, and one other man were lowered into the shaft. Because of an overhanging lip, the rest of the party had to stay on top to hoist the men out. At the bottom, Hafen and his companion failed to find the skeleton, but they did bring up a hand-forged hammer. It was later identified by Hafen as seventeenth-century vintage. Reaching out from this level were more passageways. Each ended in yet another deep pit.

Local guides accompanied this party and repeated stories of the skeleton and iron chains attached to tree trunks to form ladders. One legend proclaimed that at the bottom of the cave are two large wooden doors that guard hidden treasure.

A 1935 article published in *American Forest* magazine reviewed many of the facts about La Caverna del Oro. The article, however, added a new legend. A skeleton, hung on a wooden cross, once guarded Marble Cave near La Caverna del Oro. As the story goes, a trapper wandered near the cave, and to protect their interests, the Spaniards crucified him. For half a century, his bones remained on the cross. Members of the Fremont expedition gave the poor fellow a decent burial. The trapper's ghost haunts the cave, according to the legend.

A piece of human bone was recovered in 1959 from a pool in the cave. Another expedition found a bundle of dynamite dangling over the first pit. Someone chiseled away part of the Maltese cross, and strange lights have been seen in the vicinity of the cave.

Lloyd E. Parris, in his excellent book, *Caves of Colorado*, concludes that even now the cave resists all intruders. Everything seems to go wrong when attempts are made to explore La Caverna del Oro. Cavers become sick, or basic caving techniques are momentarily forgotten. Most attempts to solve the riddles only tend to complicate them. Only during recent years has the cave been fully explored. Many of the legends now seem believable, but what about the lost gold? Why didn't any of the expeditions find evidence of mining? Are there two doors at the bottom of the cave to guard the treasure, as one legend claims? The final chapter of La Caverna del Oro is yet to be written.

Members of a 1932 expedition into La Caverna del Oro wait at the top of the second pit. Note the wooden framework said to have been used by the Spaniards to hoist gold ore. (Denver Public Library, Western History Department)

References

Morgan, Nicolas. "Mystery Caves in Colorado." *Rocky Mountain News*, September 21, 1921.

Parris, Lloyd E. *Caves of Colorado*. Boulder, Colorado: Pruett Publishing Co., 1973, pp. 24 32, 112 116.

Wolf, Tom. *Colorado's Sangre de Cristo Mountains*. Niwot, Colorado: University Press of Colorado, 1995, pp. 63 64.

**The deadly rat game.**
(Drawing by Karen Manci)

# The Deadly Rat Game

Because "Uncle" Billy Cozens was a young man with a craving for adventure, he set out from his home in New York state around 1859, and headed for Colorado to prospect for gold. He reached Black Hawk nearly broke.

Jack Kehler operated a store located in a long, low cabin in Black Hawk. It, like everything else in town, showed signs of having been built in a great hurry. No chinking was used between the logs. This made the structure cold and drafty. In the corner of the store, Kehler had set up a bar on rough planks that spanned a couple of barrels. Assorted bottles of gin, brandy and whiskey were haphazardly placed on three plank shelves on the cabin wall behind the makeshift bar. Smoking tobacco and a few plugs of chewing tobacco also were kept on the shelves. A little tin cup on the bottom shelf held gold dust Kehler took in trade for drinks. The price for a drink was as much gold dust as the bartender could remove from the miner's pouch with two fingers in one pinch.

At the back of the store and across from the bar was a big pile of flour sacks. Kehler spread blankets on top of the pile and slept there during the night.

The rest of the store was filled with boxes and barrels containing supplies. When a new shipment arrived, Kehler would unload the merchandise into the nearest empty space. He would pry open a box of goods and sell directly from the box without moving it until it was empty.

Young Cozens entered and looked around Kehler's store-combination-bar and decided to use some of his money to buy a drink. When he paid Kehler in currency, Kehler remarked, "Hub, tenderfoot money! Must be a new arrival! When'd ye get in?"

"Uncle" Billy Cozens as a young man. After his early experiences in Black Hawk, he later became sheriff of Gilpin County and lived for many years in Central City. (Denver Public Library, Western History Department, negative F27016)

"Yes," replied Cozens, "Damn new and damn near broke, and I am looking for a job."

When Kehler found out that Cozens had worked as a carpenter, he asked, "Think you could chink up this building and make a tight job of it, young feller?"

Cozens guaranteed that if he didn't do a good job of chinking the walls, Kehler would not owe him a cent. In three days the log building was nicely chinked and tight. After being paid a liberal sum, Kehler asked, "Ever tend bar, Billy?"

After finding that Cozens knew absolutely nothing about tending bar, Kehler said, "T'aint much to it to learn. All you got to do is to keep sober when the other boys is fillin' up, and jest give'em all they want to buy so long as their dust lasts to pay for it, and don't let any whiskey go out on tick [sic]. The hours is purty long for me, and I'm needin' a clerk . . . some young feller who can tend bar and sell the groceries. If you want the job, Billy, you can have it." With this, Cozens went to work tending bar and selling groceries.

The store had a dirt floor, and rats dug tunnels under the lowest layer of logs to get inside. They also raced around the walls inside the chinking. The rats were quite numerous, and Kehler, using his expert shooting ability, picked them off as he sat on the pile of flour sacks.

One day, just as Cozens finished work, a big, fat rat ran along the top of the wall behind his head. Without warning, Kehler blew the rat to kingdom come, and the blood spattered all over Cozens. The fact that Cozens jumped off the ground just amused Kehler. He laughed and said, "Nuthin' to get nervous about, Billy, I was jest killin' a rat!" He then laid back on the flour sacks and laughed.

Several days passed, and Kehler once again used his revolver to suddenly blast another rat from behind the bar where Cozens was serving. Cozens again jumped, and Kehler said, "No need to jump, Billy! I was jest killin' a rat!"

A week went by without any rats getting behind the bar. As Cozens set a gin bottle back on the shelf, Kehler shot another rat. The rat, however, was on the same shelf, and the bullet broke the gin bottle held between Cozens' fingers. He not only jumped but yelled at his employer. Again Kehler only laughed and said, "Nuthin' to be bothered about! I had to kill the rat!"

Cozens also was familiar with the use of firearms and had enough of Kehler's deadly rat game. One afternoon, as Kehler dozed on his flour-sack bed, Cozens spotted a big, fat rat running along the upper log. He waited until the rat was right over Kehler's head, took aim and fired. The bullet was a little low and clipped a piece out of Kehler's ear. He woke up instantly and reached for the remainder of his ear. He first looked at his blood-covered hand, then back at Cozens holding the smoking revolver.

The St. James Methodist Church in Central City, the first Protestant church constructed in Colorado, was built by Cornish stonemasons. Construction started in 1864, but the building was not completed until 1872. (Kenneth Jessen)

you." They also called everyone by some endearing term, such as "my son" or "my beauty." Using "thee" for "you," they might inquire, " 'Ow are thee gettin' on there, my son?"

The Cornish became known as "Cousin Jacks" at the Colorado mining camps. Their talent as miners was exceptional, and when a mine foreman was impressed with his Cornish miner, he would ask if there were any others like him back in Cornwall. The Cornishman usually would know of other miners wanting to leave the old country and might answer, "My cousin Jack be a very good miner and 'ee should like a new job."

One Cornishman took an owl for a flat-face chicken and wanted to purchase it from the bartender. (Kenneth Jessen)

The miners reasoned that foremen would be more apt to accept another member of the miner's family, where in fact, the "Cousin Jack" the miner had in mind might not be related at all. Because the men were known as "Cousin Jacks," it seemed fitting that the Cornish women were known as "Cousin Jennies."

Some of the mining camp saloons offered a free drink to the first patron of the day. On a cold, snowy morning, two "Cousin Jacks" arrived simultaneously at the door of a saloon that had a particular offer to entice early drinking customers. The owner gave both a free drink. The drink warmed their souls after their brisk walk from home and was so fine that the Cornishmen decided to buy another.

As was their custom, they alternated paying for the drinks, and so it went on through the morning. Naturally, the more they consumed, the more they thought of facing the cold walk to the mine, and a long day underground became less attractive. The two men debated on whether to go to work and couldn't arrive at any conclusion. One of them came up with an idea to solve this dilemma and said, "Partner, I'll tell thee what we'll do. We shall go out and throw a rock, and if 'ee stays up, we shall go to work!"

One "Cousin Jack" was forced to help his wife with a boarding house and bemoaned the high cost of food in the mining camp. To get away from the house for a while, he decided to try a brand new saloon. A stuffed owl was mounted in back of the bar as a novelty item. The first thing that caught the eye of the Cornishman was that owl. Apparently he had never seen this type of bird in the old country and asked the bartender, "Ere, my son, 'ow much is that flat-face chicken up there?"

The bartender replied, "That's no flat-face chicken, that's an owl."

Misunderstanding the reply, the Cornishman retorted sharply, "I don't care 'ow hold 'ee is, 'ee's good enough for boarders!"

As more Cornish miners joined the ranks of the mining camps, an expression came forth: "Wherever there is a hole in the earth, you will find a Cornishman at the bottom of it."

One Colorado Cornish miner claimed he worked so high in altitude that he could hear the angels sing and down so deep in the earth that he could hear the Chinese doing their dishes.

Methodist Bishop Donald H. Tippett, who lived in Central City, came in contact with many Cornish miners. He recalled that the camp was so crowded that the miners were forced to sleep three to a bed. Whenever one of them wanted to turn over he shouted, "Ready?" The second man would repeat, "Ready."

The third man would then say, "Turn." All three would then turn over in unison.

One night, three Cornish miners were rather drunk and wandered into the St. James Methodist Church during a revival meeting. Finding a pew at the back, the trio sat down just as the evangelist was warming the crowd up with a hymn. The verse went, "The judgment day is coming, are you ready?" The preacher repeated in a loud voice, "Are you ready?" The miners found it irresistible and joined in with a shout, "Turn!"

The Cornish miners had many superstitions and strongly believed that a woman in a mine was bad luck. Whistling in a mine could also bring bad luck. Greatly feared were the "knockers." They were bigheaded, small-eyed, wide-mouthed, evil spirits that could vanish in a puff of smoke. A "knocker" stood about two feet tall, and they were believed to be the spirits of dead miners. They wore tiny miner's boots and colorful shirts. The "knockers" used small hammers and picks to torment the Cornish miners while they were at work. It was very bad luck to run across one of these creatures in a dark mine passage. Mine explosions and cave-ins were blamed on the "knockers" by the Cornish.

References

Friggens, Paul. "The Curious 'Cousin Jacks'." *American West*, Vol. XV, No. 6 (November/December 1978), pp. 4 7, 62, 63.

Friggens, Myriam. *Tales, Trails and Tommy Knockers*. Boulder: Johnson Publishing Co., 1979, pp. 93 94.

Murphy, Michael. "When the Cousin Jacks Came to Central City." *Denver Post Empire Magazine*, July 5, 1981, pp. 14 18.

Thompson, J. T. "Cousin Jack Stories." *Colorado Magazine*, Vol. XXXV, No. 3 (July 1958), pp. 187 192.

Big Phil, the cannibal.
(Drawing by Karen Manci)

# Indian Eater Big Phil

Big Phil, also known as Mountain Phil, was both gigantic and repulsive. He became one of Denver's favorite storytellers, using his harsh voice and large hands to make gestures illustrating his stories. During a tale, he would pause to stroke the ears of his huge dog. He was forever bumming those in Denver's saloons for free drinks. When really liquored up, he told of devouring both of his Indian wives, an Indian guide and a Frenchman. And if these stories didn't frighten a person, his dog did.

James A. Gordon was one of Denver's early criminals, having killed several people. On July 18, 1860, Gordon shot a bartender for no reason, and two days later, entered the Denver Hall. In it sat Big Phil. For some reason, Gordon did not like Big Phil. Gordon drew and fired at Big Phil a couple of times as Big Phil exited the establishment at top speed.

Big Phil was known all over the West from Yellowstone to Arizona among mountain men and Indians alike. Big Phil's real name was Charles Gardner. He was sent to prison for a crime committed in 1844 in his hometown of Philadelphia. He had killed a Catholic priest. Gardner escaped and headed west to the Rocky Mountains where he trapped and lived off the land. The Indians were impressed with his size and strength, and they considered him as being from another world. Much of the time, Big Phil lived with the Indians. During times when no white man was safe from Indians, Big Phil traveled freely and periodically acted as a liaison officer for the government. One of his camps was located in an Arapaho settlement along Cherry Creek at the future site of Denver.

One winter, Big Phil and his Indian guide were sent by Gen. William S. Harney from Fort Craig, New Mexico, to Fort Laramie, Wyoming, with dispatches. A blizzard struck, and after trudging through deep, blowing snow, Big Phil and the Indian lost the trail. Their provisions gave out, but the two continued.

As Big Phil later recalled:

Ain't had a bite to eat as our grub gives out, and with snow a foot deep on the ground, cain't even see any game. I begins to feel holler in the flanks. So after livin' for 'bout five days on nothin' but wishes, I starts a-gittin' mad and watchin' the old Injun. I note him sizin' me up like I does him. I tasted man meat afore, so I figures to myself, 'Injun grub.' The next day about the time evenin' rolls around, and with my stomach rubbin' agin' my holler ribs, I can't get that Injun off my mind. So after we gits limpin' along for the day, I slips up behind him with my gun already cocked just as he's gittin' his roll from his hoss. Bang. He kicks for a minute or two. It's already dark and I hacks off one arm and fills up on raw meat as there ain't no wood for fire. I knows I cain't travel far without grub, so I hacks off the other arm and the two legs off at the hip bone, which I packs on the extra pony that I takes from the dead Injun, and starts out once agin' the next mornin'. They last me another week when I rolls into the fort.

Meanwhile at the fort, Big Phil and the Indian were weeks overdue. Then one day, Big Phil was spotted approaching the fort alone. He was asked what became of his Indian guide. Big Phil pulled a black and shriveled foot from his pack, then tossed the gruesome thing away and said, "There, damn ye, I needn't have to gnaw on you anymore."

*Rocky Mountain News* founder and editor William Byers asked about the taste of human flesh, and Big Phil answered that the head, hands and feet, when thoroughly cooked, tasted good, not unlike pork. But the other portions of the body did not suit the cannibal because they were too gristly and tough.

Kit Carson and his companions came through what was to become the city of Denver and found Big Phil living in a tipi with his squaw, Kloock. Carson asked Big Phil to trap for him, but said that none of his men wanted to stay with him (or for that matter, walk ahead of him on a trail). The following spring, one of Carson's men, Charlie Jones, stopped by to see if Big Phil needed supplies. Upon his return to Carson's camp, Jones reported, "It seems Mountain Phil has been faring better than any of us, for he had been able to kill his meat at camp, thereby saving him the trouble of having to get out and hunt for it." Jones continued, "Boys, if I should tell you what I know about Mountain Phil, you never would believe it, but as sure as you live, he had killed his squaw and eaten most of her."

It is generally believed that Big Phil was killed in Montana around 1874.

**References**

Hafen, LeRoy R. "Mountain Men 'Big Phil', the Cannibal."
   *Colorado Magazine,* Vol. XIII, No. 2 (March, 1936), pp. 53 58.
Smiley, Jerome C. *History of Denver.* Denver: Old American Publishing
   Company, (originally published in 1901), p. 343.
White, Philip W. "Twelve Colorado Characters." *1967 Denver Westerner's
   Brand Book,* Vol. XXIII. Denver: The Westerners, 1968, pp.      276 277.
Zamonski, Stanley W., and Teddy Keller. *The '59er's.* Frederick, Colorado:
   Platte N Press, 1961, pp. 47 48.

Pickled head in jar.

(Drawing by Kenneth Jessen)

# The Pickled Skull Mystery

A half-dozen Texas Rangers got wind of a rich gold strike in South Park during 1863. This prompted the Rangers to ride north to check things over. Their destination was the new Colorado mining camp of Montgomery, located at the foot of Hoosier Pass and at the headwaters of the South Platte River. Montgomery had already hit its peak by this time and became the largest community in the entire South Park region.

One evening, the Rangers decided to explore the foothills. During their ride, they spotted an encampment of Ute Indians belonging to Chief Colorow. Low on rations, the Texans boldly rode into the Indian camp. Colorow had mixed feelings about white men but decided to help the Rangers by giving them some fresh meat and assigning them a place to camp.

The Rangers took note of the Indian ponies. During a dinner of fresh antelope steaks provided by the Indians, the Rangers discussed the question of stealing some of the ponies.

At dawn, Colorow's braves got ready to organize a hunting party. Boys were sent to find the swiftest mounts from the herd and quickly discovered that a dozen of their best ponies were missing. Their Texan guests also were gone, and the ashes of their campfire were nearly cold.

The hunting party quickly switched to war paint and took after the Texan horse thieves. The trail led past Fairplay and into heavy timber. The Rangers knew the Indians would follow and took a circuitous route back toward Montgomery. The Indians were excellent trackers and soon caught up with the ungrateful Rangers. The two parties fought in a gulch near Mount Silver Heels.

Little is known about the battle. One of the Rangers died in the conflict, and his name was listed only as "John Smith." The

Indians stripped "John Smith" of his clothes but left his scalp. No trace was found of the other Rangers, and it is presumed they escaped.

Doc Bailey of Montgomery was a jovial physician, but most of his practice was confined to staggering between one of the town's saloons and his cabin. He owned a drugstore and a shoe store in Montgomery. He was also an avid hunter. A few days after the Ute-Ranger battle, Bailey was hunting along the base of Mount Silver Heels when he suddenly brought his horse to a stop. He could see a white object stretched out on the side of a rock, and it looked human. He rode over to the still form just

Montgomery, located south of Hoosier Pass, was not much to look at, as evidenced by this 1867 photograph. (Colorado Historical Society)

as the others in his party arrived. Dismounting, Bailey drew his hunting knife and tested its edge on his thumb. He remarked to his friends that he had always wanted a human head to dissect and study. Much to the horror of his companions, he sawed off the head of "John Smith," leaving the rest of the corpse to rot.

After he arrived back at his office, Doc Bailey got out a large pickle jar and submerged his trophy in pickling solution. So that all could see his prize possession, he placed the head in his office window. Needless to say, those passing by found the sight of the head in a pickle jar repulsive. It wasn't long before some citizen stole the head, placed it in a gunny sack and dropped it into an abandoned mine shaft.

Long after "John Smith" and the story of the battle between the Rangers and the Ute Indians was forgotten, two miners purchased an old claim near the ghost town of Montgomery. The men pumped the water out of the shaft and began to clean out the debris to begin mining operations. While shoveling out the mud, one of them hit something round that was covered with rotting cloth. With the mud and cloth removed, the object clearly was a human skull. The discovery was a mystery; the abandoned shaft yielded no bones. Fortunately, an old-timer remembered the story of Doc Bailey and solved the pickled skull mystery.

### References
Bair, Everett. *This Will Be an Empire.* New York: Pageant Press, 1959, pp. 3 35.
Brown, Robert L. *Ghost Towns of the Colorado Rockies.* Caldwell, Idaho: Caxton Printers, 1977, pp. 224 225.

John Q. A. Rollins played an incredible billiards match with Charles Cook and won $11,000 in the process. The match lasted 33 hours. Later in his life, Rollins made a fortune in gold mining. Rollins Pass and Rollinsville are named after this Colorado pioneer. (Colorado Historical Society)

# The Billiards Game

John Q. A. Rollins was tall and broad. He arrived in Denver in 1866 at a time when many who won fortunes one day lost them the next. About two o'clock in the afternoon, Rollins stopped at a billiards hall over Brendlinger's cigar store at Blake and F streets. A banker named Charles A. Cook struck up a conversation with Rollins. The two men talked about mining, real estate and a variety of subjects. Eventually, their conversation turned to billiards. Cook, confident of his skill, laughed at Rollins when the latter said he could beat him. Rollins challenged Cook and gave away 20 points in each game of 100. Cook responded to the challenge by betting $400 on each game. In addition, the two men agreed that they would play until one of them gave up. At that point, the individual who quit would have to forfeit $1,000.

The men shed their coats and selected their cues. Play began at about three, and Rollins took an immediate lead despite the 20-point handicap. Cook seemed to have unusually bad luck as the balls broke the wrong way. He continued to play, letting nothing disturb his concentration. As darkness came, lamps were lit. Amid cigar smoke, the game continued.

Rumor of the billiards match spread through Denver, and the hall was soon filled to capacity with spectators. Marked with chalk, the floor served as a score pad that everyone could see. By 10 o'clock in the evening, the two antagonists were still at it. Money was flowing steadily from Cook's pockets as he lost game after game. At midnight, however, Rollins began to fatigue, and the game swung in favor of Cook. As Cook smelled revenge, he raised the stakes to $800 per game, and Rollins agreed.

Interest in the game continued on through the night, and Cook continued to win until an hour before dawn. Then Rollins got his second wind, and the tide swung the other way. Cook struggled against the odds as the chalk marks on the floor piled up against him.

The game continued on through the following day, and some merchants closed their businesses to see the match. Cook would occasionally make a brilliant shot, but the run of luck was decidedly against him. By noon, Rollins was several thousand dollars ahead as he calculated the angle required for every shot. In contrast, Cook took what he could get and aimed for direct results.

After 32 hours of continuous play, the adversaries looked as pale as the tips of their cues. Their appearance clearly showed the strain on their nerves. Cook trailed by a staggering $12,000, but he continued to play to win. Rollins was weary and dragged his body slowly around the billiards table after each shot. Finally, one hour before midnight, Rollins gave up, forfeited the $1,000, and took the $11,000 Cook owed him. The players shook hands, went to bed and never made any effort to renew the match.

Rollins later made a fortune in gold mining in Gilpin County. He invested in a stage line, salt works in South Park, a toll road over Rollins Pass and founded the small town of Rollinsville. By 1879, Rollins owned 20,000 linear feet of gold-bearing veins, 300 acres of placer gold-mining deposits and 2,000 acres of farm land. Cook also became a wealthy man as he continued his banking career.

**References**
Rollins, John Q. A., Jr. "John Q.A. Rollins, Colorado Builder." *Colorado Magazine*, XVI, No. 3 (May 1939), pp. 110 118.

# Captain Sam Heads to the Pacific

During the exploration of the West, it was hoped that a navigable water route could be found to the Pacific Ocean. This was an objective of Maj. John Wesley Powell's 1869 expedition on the Colorado River. But there were also other less well known explorers seeking a way to reach California and the Pacific Ocean by water. "Captain" Samuel Adams was one of them. He demonstrated how far a man could get on nothing but gall and the gift of gab.

Samuel Adams offered Major Powell his services. Adams claimed he had firsthand knowledge of the Colorado River. He also told Powell he was authorized by the secretary of war to explore the great river. Powell quickly sent this fast-tongued "authority" on his merry way.

In July 1869, Adams made friends with the people of Breckenridge. The small mining town was located deep in the Colorado Rockies on the Blue River. He found some individuals willing to listen and invest in a "sure thing." The plan was simple. Adams was to head up his own scientific expedition to float down the Blue River to the Colorado River and on to California and the Pacific Ocean.

His backers constructed four boats out of green lumber, the only material available in Breckenridge. The boats were open, with no decking or air compartments. Adams enlisted 10 of the most able-bodied "seamen" the mining town could muster. The expedition members were equipped with muzzle-loading rifles, 200 rounds of ammunition and ample food supplies for the long journey. The ladies of Breckenridge made a banner for the flagship that read, "Western Colorado to California, Greetings."

Some of the details of the proposed trip were a little fuzzy in the mind of "Captain" Adams. For example, it was not clear

"Captain" Samuel Adams attempted to find a water-level route from Breckenridge using the Blue River to the Colorado River and on to the Pacific Ocean. For his effort, he was branded "a preposterous, twelve-gauge, hundred-proof, kiln-dried, officially notarized fool." (Colorado Historical Society)

to Adams just how far it was to California by water. He did know that Breckenridge was nearly two miles above sea level and that he would have to lose that distance vertically to reach the Pacific Ocean.

There were speeches and cheers as the town gave Adams and his crew a big send-off. Two of the four boats entered the river about two-and-a-half miles below Breckenridge, while the other two boats were hauled by wagon to a second launch area farther downstream. This strategy may have been to determine if the boats were seaworthy prior to committing all of them to the river.

During the first day, the Adams expedition traveled nine miles. The captain made observations in his ship's log as to the width and depth of the Blue River. In most instances, he left blanks for the figures he planned to fill in later. That evening, the party dined on homemade bread. Adams reported smooth sailing the first day, except that his boat was upset twice.

The next day the two boats that had been sent overland arrived, and there was a new launching celebration. Judge Marshall Silverthorn made a speech and presented "Captain" Adams with a dog. What value the dog could have been to the expedition, or even if it survived the journey, remains a mystery.

On July 14, 1869, the experiences of the expedition gave its members an uncomfortable hint of what was in store for them. They swirled around a bend in the river and entered some rapids. In seconds, all but the members in the last boat were tossed into the ice cold water and were left hanging on the boulders in midstream. The "instruments" (whatever they were) and the captain's box of papers floated down the turbulent Blue.

On Sunday, July 18, one of the expedition members was sent back to Breckenridge for more "instruments" and some matches. Because of the dunking, dry matches were needed to build a fire to dry equipment and clothes. The rest of the party stayed and repaired the boats. Soon, the first signs of failing enthusiasm surfaced. Adams recorded in his diary that the party contributed $30 to a Mr. Ricker and sent him home as a "common nuisance."

Once again, expedition members pushed their boats into the Blue and continued their journey. Adams said he would go on even if all others abandoned him. After a short distance, one of the boats collided with a rock and was demolished. The second set of "instruments" was lost, and Adams claimed he was now at a scientific disadvantage. His entry for the day was, "Distance by water from Breckenridge, (blank) miles."

On the 22nd, four of the hardy explorers gave up and returned to Breckenridge. Dissension set in. The following day a party member was temporarily missing, and Adams had to man his own boat alone. He swamped it only once, and this was attributable to a fallen tree across the river. For the last eight miles to the confluence of the Blue and Colorado rivers, the water was smooth. The expedition was now 55 miles and 12 days from their starting point, but minus five members and one boat.

For one entire week there was a gap in the captain's diary. Possibly his pencil floated off to join his "instruments." On July 30, the party took to the water once again, and after just five miles they camped. Adams dispatched two members to Hot Sulphur Springs to bring back newspapers and more matches.

Farther down the Colorado River, fixed lines had to be used to keep the boats from capsizing in the swift current. Adams told the other party members that he had never seen the Colorado River so rough before. Since Adams probably had never been down the river before, he spoke the truth. One of the boats swung out of control on its line and filled with water. The party lost 100 pounds of bacon, a sack of flour, an axe, a saw, a small oven, two canteens of salt, 35 pounds of coffee and a few other items. After arriving at the bottom of this stretch of river, the party took stock of what provisions remained, and it wasn't much.

On August 3, they constructed paddles and used fixed lines to descend another stretch of rapids. It took an entire day to travel 300 yards. The only good thing that happened was the recovery of a slab of bacon. They had now entered the Gore Canyon, and as it got progressively deeper, the river became a succession of rapids and waterfalls. Retreat seemed impossible.

One of the boats was swamped on August 5, and it took all morning to free it before the expedition could continue. A line

At the time "Captain" Samuel Adams launched his boats on the Blue River in 1869, Breckenridge was a small, rugged mining town. Many of the town's residents helped finance the expedition. (Colorado Historical Society)

attached to that same boat broke in the afternoon, and it was released to the untamed river. The boat disappeared beneath the foaming water. It required four days of hard work to negotiate another three-quarters of a mile of river. In the process, nearly all of the food was lost. Now only one boat remained with which to reach California.

Adams may have lacked common sense and ability, but he did reason that the faster the river dropped toward the sea, the sooner he would reach smooth water. On August 6, the party threw away all extra clothing and equipment to strip down for the passage to the Pacific Ocean in one vessel. They struggled from portage to portage, but finally the boat was swamped. Its line broke, and it was dashed to splinters on the rocks by the force of the mighty Colorado River.

"Captain" Samuel Adams proved his dedication, and he and his five companions constructed a raft and continued their journey. Finally, though, three members took a look at the pounding rapids, mused over their remaining food and abandoned the trip. Adams and his loyal explorers packed their goods farther down the canyon. As they hiked along, they passed rocks strewn with the remains of their boats, supplies, "instruments" and clothing.

On August 10, a larger raft was built from driftwood, and the party took to the water once again. After three miles, the river delivered them straight into a boulder, dashing all hope of continuing. Adams reluctantly gave up on August 13, and set aside his quest for a water-level route to the Pacific.

Later, Adams tendered a $20,000 claim to the U.S. government for services rendered in exploring the Colorado River. All attempts to collect this and a lesser amount were rejected since the expedition was unauthorized. History recorded that Adams was "a preposterous, twelve-gauge, hundred-proof, kiln-dried, officially notarized fool, or else he was one of the most wildly incompetent scoundrels who ever lived."

### References
Bueler, Gladys R. *Colorado's Colorful Characters*. Boulder, Colorado: Pruett Publishing Co., 1981, p. 45.
Eberhart, Perry. *Guide to the Colorado Ghost Towns and Mining Camps*. Denver: Sage Books, 1959, p. 141.
Gilliland, Mary Ellen. *Summit*. Silverthorne, Colorado: Alpenrose Press, 1980, pp. 267 268.

# Gold Bricks for Sale

Doc Baggs was a con man, pure and simple, and as his specialty, he only picked on prominent people. Baggs knew that once taken, out of sheer embarrassment, such people were unlikely to tell the authorities. Baggs chose his intended victims with the utmost care and always struck for big money. He is credited with originating the gold-brick game.

Among Baggs's most extraordinary exploits was the sale of two gold bricks to a couple of San Diego mining men. The victims paid $25,000 for their "education" in the gold-brick scam. Gold was a magic metal during the Colorado boom years in the late 1800s, and the prospect of owning a solid brick of the precious metal was irresistible to many suckers. The brick was, in reality, nothing more that a common brick covered with a thin layer of gold to allow it to pass a surface assay test.

Baggs also dealt in mining property. He could converse about ore, assay results, mineralization and other technical matters. He dressed in authentic miner's clothing to give the impression he knew firsthand about mining. In this way, he got people interested in purchasing shares in his plentiful underground wealth.

Performing these acts often required elaborate staging. Baggs rich-looking office contained the finest furniture. An immense safe appeared to be built into one wall. No less than 10 square feet, its massive doors were left open so that the victim could peer into its inner depths to view shelving, boxes and other items while discussing some deal with Doc. Fancy lettering, delicate flowers and elaborate emblems were added on the safe to impart the feeling of integrity.

The safe was actually a clever painting. In case of an unexpected visit by the police, the safe could be removed from the wall in seconds. It was a mosaic of numbered, thin wooden panels each about the size of a cigar box lid. The painting was on a fabric placed on the panels. The entire painting could be folded up quickly and carried out of the building or stored.

When a potential sucker entered the office, Baggs would stand in front of the safe. The rest of the room contained solid oak counters and the traditional railing with a gate. The glass in the door leading into the room might be inscribed with "Private" or "Superintendent" or "Manager," depending on the occasion. The door was constructed so that it could be moved quickly into a hiding place built into one of the walls. Sometimes, the con required a row of clerks sitting on high wooden stools behind a counter. For this, he would hire fellow con men to work on thick papier-mâché ledgers.

After the sucker was separated from his money, Baggs would fold up his safe, tuck it under his arm and walk out of the room. Other props were tucked into hiding places, the doors were slid back into cavities in the walls and the "clerks" would follow Doc out into the street.

One of Doc's men was usually assigned to follow the victim. If the victim headed to the police, Doc's man would try to head him off and even offer to return part of the money. The objective was to avoid trouble with the law.

The victim might frantically get the Denver police and lead them up to where he was sure Baggs' office was located. The victim might even enter without knocking, pushing the door open only to reveal a room furnished as a woman's bedroom. At this point, the police might attach another meaning to the victim's story.

Michael Spangler, a Denver lawman, tried to put an end to Baggs' activities by arresting him on the charge of "bunco steering." He was quick to point out to the court that even in a very large dictionary, the term "bunco steering" did not exist and that no such term appeared in Denver's statutes.

Spangler then assigned Emil Auspity to tail Baggs. When he entered into one of his convincing routines for the benefit of a potential sucker, Auspity interrupted. The deputy warned the victim he was dealing with Doc Baggs, the most notorious confidence man in Denver. Baggs was helpless against this type of harassment and began to use a variety of disguises. It became a game for Baggs to dress up in different outfits. After completing a scam, he might identify himself to the deputy just to torment him. To vary his trick, he got one of his cronies to give Auspity false tips as to his identity for that day. Many innocent citizens were falsely accused of being the famous con artist, much to Baggs' delight.

Prior to leaving Denver for good, Doc Baggs sold a gold brick to H. M. Smith of Leadville for $20,000. Smith was a banker and took the bait handed him by Baggs, who claimed that the gold brick was purchased from a poor Mexican living in a shack. One of his men played the role of the Mexican who claimed the brick was part of the loot taken in a train robbery. Smith had the brick analyzed two years later, and the fraud was exposed.

**References**

Collier, William Ross, and Edwin Victor Westrate. *The Reign of Soapy Smith.* New York: Doubleday, 1935, pp. 27 29.

Robertson, Frank G., and Beth Kay Harris. *Soapy Smith: King of the Frontier Con Men.* New York: Hastings House, 1961, pp. 3 37.

From left to right: James T. Gardner, Richard D. Cotter, William H. Brewer and Clarence King. All were members of the Fortieth Parallel Survey and were surprised when diamonds were discovered in an area they had studied carefully.

(U. S. Geological Survey)

# Colorado's Diamond Field

The history of Colorado is filled with stories of thousands of men walking and riding horseback through virgin forests, crossing crystal clear mountain streams, poking into every cranny of exposed rock and searching for quick riches. The state had not been fully explored by the 1870s, and was still full of mystery in the minds of those willing to endure many hardships. The men attracted to the frontier were not above any means of making a quick dollar. Practically every visitor to the state was looking for a pot of gold, and it didn't take long before some of them capitalized on the excessive greed of others.

A pair of dirty, bearded, disheveled prospectors came to San Francisco one foggy morning in 1872. Philip Arnold and John Slack looked like they had run out of luck as they waited near the front door of a prominent bank. When the first employee arrived, they asked to be let in. The pair looked up and down the street and were wary of anyone who might be watching. Once inside, Arnold cautiously pulled out a small leather pouch. The two men asked the employee if it could be kept in the bank's vault. The employee was curious about the pouch's contents and asked what it contained. Arnold and his partner scanned the bank's empty lobby as if to seek out someone in hiding. The employee swore he would never tell another soul about the pouch. The prospectors poured the contents on a table, and much to the amazement of the employee, the pouch contained raw diamonds.

Arnold and Slack vanished into the San Francisco fog and remained out of sight for several weeks. They counted on human nature, and sure enough, the employee showed the sack of diamonds to the bank's officers. They, in turn, contacted some wealthy investors. A frantic search was made for the prospectors.

Arnold and Slack came out of hiding, and at first, they resisted any offers to let others in on the location of their diamond field. Finally, they reluctantly agreed to be a part of a new company called the New York and San Francisco Mining and Commercial Company. Their newfound colleagues paid them $600,000 (more than $6 million in today's dollars) to be let in on the secret discovery. Tiffany and Company in New York City appraised the gems and informed the investors of their great value.

One of California's best-known geologists, Henry Janin, was hired as a consultant to inspect the newly discovered diamond field. Arnold and Slack swore Janin to secrecy and took him to their find. Janin proclaimed the diamond field to be genuine. The diamond hoax was working perfectly.

News of the discovery leaked to the newspapers. To keep rumors of the diamond field alive, the prospectors appeared in Laramie, Denver and Salt Lake City during 1872. They showed their precious stones, and the newspapers spread the latest information far and wide.

Speculation held that the diamond field was located in northeastern Arizona or in New Mexico or possibly in the San Luis Valley of Colorado. Had the purported diamond field been in any of these locations, it would have been of little interest to Clarence King and his team of government geologists. But one rumor held the location to be inside the boundaries of the Fortieth Parallel Survey that King and his associates had just spent six years working to complete. The survey was an effort to discover what was in the one-hundred mile wide land grant for the Union Pacific and Central Pacific railroads. Not a single precious stone had been discovered nor had the members of the survey team found a geologic formation in which gems were likely to occur. But if they had overlooked a diamond field, their professional reputations would be on the line. Before King could issue the final report on the Fortieth Parallel Survey, he had to determine the validity of the discovery.

Samuel Emmons and fellow geologist, James Gardner, were part of King's team. On October 5, 1872, the pair took a westbound train from Battle Mountain, Nevada, where they had been doing field work. At first, they paid little attention to their fellow passengers, but at breakfast the following morning, they noticed a group of men in rough clothes. Their tan faces gave them away as returning from some type of outdoor work. By sheer coincidence, Emmons and Gardner had boarded a train with surveyors returning from the diamond field.

Fellow geologist Henry Janin was in the party. Emmons and Gardner questioned Janin and learned that he had been unable to visit the claim because he was being followed. The rest of the party took such a roundabout route they became lost. Once at the diamond field, the men were given one hour to look for jewels using only their pocket knives. The 10 surveyors returned with 280 diamonds and many rubies. The stones ranged in size from a pea to a small grain. Janin did not, however, give the slightest clue as to where the diamond field was located.

King quickly gathered a small team of government geologists to investigate the alleged diamond field. He determined that the Janin party had left the Union Pacific between Green River and Rawlins. A general description of the area where the diamonds were located was extracted from one of the members of the Janin party.

Armed with a meager amount of information, the government geologists set out to find the diamond field. They reasoned that the location was south of the railroad, at the base of a peak, and about 10 miles north of Brown's Park, placing it just south of the Colorado-Wyoming line. In October 1872, the King party, including Emmons and Gardner, left San Francisco. To avoid suspicion, their code word for diamonds was "carboniferous fossils." Upon their arrival at Fort Bridger, Wyoming, the officers and soldiers at the fort weren't surprised that the team was after "carboniferous fossils." Just as they were leaving on horseback, the post surgeon whispered into Emmons' ear,

"Bring me back a couple of solitaires, will you?" It was simply hard to keep the expedition a secret.

The weather was bitterly cold, with temperatures driven below zero by a relentless wind. The bleak, treeless expanse of prairie offered no protection or relief from the elements. The animals were worn out, and their legs became encased in balls of ice from crossing the streams. After four days, the party crossed the Green River. Finally, one of the men found a written claim signed by Henry Janin. This led them to a table rock area, and the men were encouraged by the discovery of a few diamonds and rubies. It was late in the day on November 2, 1872, and Emmons wrote in his diary, "That night we were full-believers in the verity of Janin's reports, and dreamed of the untold wealth that might be gathered."

The following morning the men came to a startling conclusion: the number of gems decreased rapidly outside the windswept table rock at the center of the claim. The frequency of occurrence was studied. There were always about one dozen rubies for every diamond found. Nature certainly doesn't maintain a ratio of precious stones. By using their sieves, the men were only able to find gems where the earth had been disturbed. Nothing more than common quartz crystals were found where the soil was untouched. The anthills gave yet another clue that the area had been salted. Some of the hills had a footprint close by and small holes had been made near the entrance produced by the ants. At the bottom of each hole, a ruby or two could be recovered, but on any other place on the hill, there were no gem stones. Anthills with no footprints yielded no gemstones.

In King's party was a middle-aged German. He was not wealthy and had never been in a place where a person could stoop down and pick up a diamond. He didn't want to leave despite the intense cold and constant wind. While he was washing dirt and occasionally pocketing a sparkler, he came across a stone that caught his eye. It filled him with wonderment since it bore the marks of the lapidary's art. He immediately called out, "Look here, Mr. King. This is the bulliest diamond field as never vas. It not only produces diamonds, but cuts them moreover also." King snatched the stone from the German's hand and everything was as clear as day: the area was salted. King hunted for more evidence and soon had proof that wholesale fraud had been committed.

A problem faced King. If he accused the prospectors of fraud when there was no fraud, his entire Fortieth Parallel Survey would be discredited, and six years of hard work would go down the drain. Henry Janin had publicly pronounced the diamond field to be real, and his reputation as a geologist was without fault. King elected to stay in the cold and wind to gather more evidence.

On the fourth day, a hole three-feet wide and 10 feet deep was dug. All of the dirt was examined, and no gems were found below the surface. The results were conclusive. King released his men, returned to San Francisco and exposed the diamond hoax. He saved many small, potential investors from losing money, and he may have saved the lives of prospectors trying to endure the winter by hunting gems in this remote part of Colorado. King was heralded as a hero and as a credit to the government survey team.

The trustees of the San Francisco and New York Mining and Commercial Company selected an investigating committee to ferret out and punish those guilty of the fraud. Everyone connected with the early history of the diamond field was sought. An accomplice of Arnold and Slack by the name of Cooper stepped forward. He admitted with noble candor that he was the author of the entire scheme. He felt he was unrightfully deprived by his welshing partners of his just share of the spoils. Salting gold and silver mines was nothing new and had been overworked. Cooper suggested to Arnold and Slack that salting a diamond field would be a pleasing variation. He told them that small, industrial-grade diamonds could be used for the task. Once the fraud was under way, Cooper was excluded from the details. His confession was motivated by revenge and was given first to the investigating committee, then to a grand jury in San Francisco.

The diamonds and other gems were purchased in bulk from dealers in London and Amsterdam. One dealer even identified a photograph of Arnold. Using $35,000 raised through the sale of some mining property, Arnold and Slack invested in industrial gemstones of the lowest quality. From that investment, a profit (after expenses) of $600,000 was reaped from the salted Colorado diamond field.

Once Arnold received his booty from the San Francisco and New York Mining and Commercial Company, he retired to his home in Elizabethtown in Hardin County, Kentucky. He purchased some fine property and had a safe installed in his home. He was surrounded by a host of relatives and friends.

After the fraud was uncovered by King, attorneys were hired to recover the money. A suit for $350,000 was brought against Arnold. He then publicly denied the charges in the *Louisville Journal* on December 20, 1872. Arnold, however, admitted his safe contained $550,000 which he said was the result of arduous labor as a prospector and miner. He was outraged that men from California were trying to take his wealth and to connect him with fraud. Arnold was quite clever and quoted Janin's report and the appraisal from Tiffany. He claimed he turned over a good diamond field to the investors, and if any salting had been done, it took place later.

Hardin County applauded Arnold's spunk for sticking up for his rights and for standing his ground unflinchingly against outside intruders. Eventually, the lawyers became convinced that not a dollar could be wrung from Arnold no matter what proof was submitted in court. From a political and legal standpoint, Arnold lived in an impenetrable fortress. To gain immunity from any further litigation, Arnold surrendered $150,000.

The way was now paved for Arnold to live out his life in luxury, but he wanted to enter the world of finance. He opened

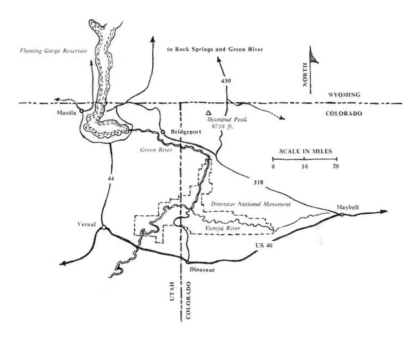

Diamond Peak, where the diamond hoax was perpetrated, is located in the extreme northwestern part of Colorado. (Map drawn by Kenneth Jessen)

a bank in Elizabethtown and did a good business based on his popularity. He loaned a rival bank $8,000, and when the collateral for this loan was not surrendered on time, Arnold brought suit. An officer of the bank, Harry Holdsworth, made some derogatory comments in a letter about Arnold's character. One thing led to another, and on a street in Elizabethtown, August 14, 1878, Arnold attacked Holdsworth with a cane, striking him a good number of solid blows.

The next day Arnold was drinking beer in Lott's Saloon when Holdsworth walked in. Arnold threw him to the floor and hit him with his fists. Holdsworth was so bloody he could not see, and he begged Arnold to stop. Only after a law officer interceded did Arnold stop his attack.

After getting cleaned up, Holdsworth went back to his bank and got a double-barreled, sawed-off shotgun. He marched back to Lott's Saloon with the weapon in the crook of his arm. Arnold was standing in front of the building, and when he saw Holdsworth, he drew his pistol and fired two shots. Both shots missed, but so did Holdsworth's first load of buckshot. Holdsworth took cover behind a tree as Arnold advanced down the street. The second discharge from the shotgun, delivered at only two feet, badly lacerated Arnold's shoulder. Holdsworth dropped his weapon and ran for his life in a hail of bullets from Arnold's gun. All of Arnold's shots missed, but a local farmer was seriously wounded by a stray round.

In February 1879, Arnold caught pneumonia and died. His wound had healed but remained painful. Many felt that the wound weakened him and brought on the pneumonia.

As for Slack, every effort was made to track him down. Arnold had all or almost all of the money. Slack could not have received much more than $30,000. It was assumed that the two men must have planned a 50-50 split. Maybe Arnold died before Slack could collect his share. Slack lived out his life as a coffin maker first in St. Louis then in White Oaks, New Mexico. He died at the age of 76.

### References

Bartlett, Richard A. *Great Surveys of the American West.* Norman, Oklahoma: University of Oklahoma Press, 1962, pp. 197 205.

"Great Diamond Swindle." *Rocky Mountain News*, January 27, 1875.

Wilkins, James H., ed. *The Great Diamond Hoax and Other Stirring Incidents in the Life of Asbury Harpending.* Norman, Oklahoma: University of Oklahoma Press, 1958, pp. 145 187.

Woodward, Bruce A. *Diamonds in the Salt.* Boulder, Colorado: Pruett Publishing Co., 1967.

# Colorado's Famous Cannibal

On November 17, 1873, a party of 21 miners left Salt Lake City for the newly discovered silver deposits in Colorado's San Juan Mountains. The party and its supply wagons arrived at the Ute Indian encampment at the junction of the Uncompahgre and Gunnison rivers (near the present-day town of Delta) on January 20, 1874. Ouray, chief of the Utes, advised the party not to continue into the mountains until spring because of severe weather and deep snow.

Some of the men took the advice of the wise chief and were given food by the Indians. Alferd Packer, however, was in a hurry to continue the journey and to be among the first to stake his claim. He told others in the party that he knew the country and persuaded five men to follow him. They left the Ute Indians on February 9, with provisions for 10 days. Some 65 days later in a blinding snowstorm, Packer walked into the Los Piños Indian Agency (about 25 miles south of the present town of Gunnison). He was alone. Gen. Charles Adams welcomed him, and when offered breakfast, Packer turned away at the sight of food. When questioned, Packer claimed that he had traveled through the mountains subsisting on rose buds and roots. He carried a Winchester rifle but claimed it did him little good since game was scarce. He also told the general that after he became ill, his companions abandoned him. General Adams continued to question Packer about the probable fate of his companions. The vivid descriptions of his suffering in the mountains awakened the sympathy of the entire agency.

After resting for a few days, Packer went over Cochetopa Pass to Saguache, which was the nearest settlement at the time. He went on a drinking binge and spent a good deal of money in the process. He also displayed his money to others, yet he claimed he was penniless when he began the trip from the Ute Indian encampment.

A second party also ignored Chief Ouray's advice and headed up the Gunnison River. The first member of this party finally reached the Los Piños Agency after suffering a great deal in the deep snow and cold. The man's name was Lutzenheiser, and he told General Adams that they managed to kill some game to keep from starving.

After hearing about Alferd Packer, especially how he had turned down food upon arrival at the agency, Lutzenheiser aroused the suspicions of General Adams. The feeling was that Packer probably murdered his companions and robbed them. Lutzenheiser also suspected that Packer's Winchester rifle belonged to old man Swan, a member of his party. General Adams brought Packer back to the agency to act as a guide in the hunt for his lost companions.

One of the Indians discovered what appeared to be a piece of human flesh not too far from the agency along the trail used by Packer. It was now feared that Packer not only killed his companions but lived off of their flesh. When confronted with the evidence, Packer admitted that he was the only surviving member of his party. He claimed that the others had been killed, one after the other.

Under oath, in the presence of others from the party that traveled up the Gunnison River, Packer was forced to make a statement. He said that after running out of supplies, the party wandered for several days in the mountains. Packer left camp to gather firewood, and when he returned, old man Swan had been killed by his companions. The others were sitting around the campfire roasting his flesh. General Adams was visibly shaken by this vivid account.

After staying a day, Packer said that the remaining members of the party left the camp taking with them a supply of Swan's flesh. Humphreys died after four or five days, and they ate his flesh to stay alive. One day, Packer said he was out again

Alferd Packer was found guilty of the premeditated murder of his five companions. His guilt always has been doubted by some, but by his own admission, he did live on the remains of his companions until he found his way out of the mountains. (Colorado Historical Society)

gathering firewood, and when he returned, he found Miller dead. George Noon and Wilson Bell claimed they killed him accidentally, but Packer knew he had been killed intentionally since it had been agreed previously that Miller should be the next man sacrificed. He was a stout German, but he was sick and hampered travel. The three remaining men cooked parts of Miller's flesh. Later on, Bell shot Noon, and Packer and Bell lived off of his flesh.

Packer continued with his story and said he camped with Bell under a large spruce tree near Lake San Cristobal (above what later became the town of Lake City). Both men were hungry. Each man took opposite sides of the tree. During the still of the night, Bell tried to kill Packer with the butt of his rifle. The blow missed, and Bell, knowing he was trapped, exclaimed, "Kill me just as I intended to kill you." Packer did just that and lived off of Bell's flesh for several days before making his way to the Indian agency.

General Adams insisted that Packer guide a party of men into the mountains to verify this story. Adams promised Packer that if his story agreed with what they found, he would be released. Packer traced his trail for a while, but when he arrived at the Lake Fork of the Gunnison River leading to Lake San Cristobal, he claimed he was lost. The party found nothing and returned to the agency. Packer was placed in irons and taken to a primitive log jail in Saguache.

A second search party was sent out to find Packer's companions. They discovered two camps near Lake San Cristobal. Evidently one camp was where the entire party stopped, but the other camp was made by one man. It was obvious the second camp had been occupied for several weeks. It had a primitive shelter constructed of branches and a neat fireplace built of flat rocks. Speculation was that Packer had killed his companions and had thrown their bodies into a nearby beaver pond. By cutting through the beaver dam, the pond was partially drained, but no trace could be found of the missing men.

An artist for *Harpers Weekly* was on vacation in the Lake City area in August 1874, and came upon a dense grove of spruce trees at the foot of a steep bluff near the banks of the Lake Fork of the Gunnison River. He was horrified to find the partially decomposed bodies of five men. The bodies of four

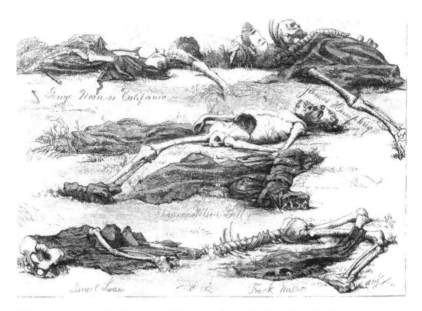

John A. Randolph discovered the remains of Alferd Packer's five companions near the present-day town of Lake City. He was a member of a sketching party roaming the West, drawing pastoral scenes. These dramatic sketches appeared in *Harper's Weekly*. (Denver Public library, Western History Department)

men were lying side by side and the fifth body was nearby. The heads of the men were cut open, and blanket fibers were embedded in the wounds as though the men had been killed while sleeping. One body (later identified as that of Miller) was missing its head, and chunks of flesh had been sliced off the chest and thighs. Flesh had been hacked from at least one other body as well. The news of this discovery reached Saguache just three days after Alferd Packer escaped from the log jail.

After nine years of freedom, Packer was spotted at Fort Fetterman in Wyoming. He was living under the assumed name of John Schwartz. One of the original members of the party to journey up the Gunnison River identified him and notified authorities.

On April 13, 1883, in the Lake City courthouse, Packer was

found guilty of premeditated murder and was sentenced to die by hanging on May 19. His first confession made at the Los Piños Agency was inconsistent with later confessions. According to his original story, the bodies should have been spread out among several campsites. Various witnesses testified that he had quite a bit of money with him in Saguache. A murder for money motive was emphasized by the prosecution. Packer was actually tried only for Swan's murder on the grounds that this alone would be enough to send him to the gallows. This was Hinsdale County's first death sentence and the first time in Colorado a man had been convicted of murder connected with cannibalism.

A certain humorous twist came when presiding Judge Melville B. Gerry allegedly delivered the following stern rebuke at the conclusion of the trial:

> Packer, ye man-eatin' son of a bitch, they was seven dimmycrats in Hinsdale County and ye eat five of 'em, God damn ye! I sentins ye to be hanged by the neck until ye're dead, dead, dead...as a warnin' ag'in reducing the dimmycratic populashun in the state.
>
> Judge Gerry actually never said anything of the kind. The statement was based on an exaggerated version of comments by Larry Dolan, an Irish saloon keeper in Lake City. But the statement has been a source of amusement for many years.

Judge Gerry did, however, make the following descriptive statement to Alferd Packer at the close of his trial:

> In 1874 you, in company with five companions, passed through the beautiful mountain valley where stands the town of Lake City.
>
> At the time the hand of man had not marred the beauties of nature. The picture was fresh from the hands of the

great Artist who created it. You and your companions camped at the base of a grand old mountain, in sight of the place you now stand, on the banks of a stream as pure and beautiful as ever traced the finger of God upon the bosom of the earth. Your every surrounding was calculated to impress your heart and nature with the omnipotence of Deity and...the helplessness of your own feeble life. In this goodly favored spot you conceived your murderous designs. You and your victims had had a weary march, and when the shadows of the mountain fell upon your little party and night drew her sable curtain around you, your unsuspecting victims lay down on the ground and were soon lost in the sleep of the weary; and when thus sweetly unconscious of danger from any quarter, and particularly from you, their trusted companion, you cruelly and brutally slew them all.

Whether your murderous hand was guided by the misty light of the moon, or the flickering blaze of the campfire, you only can tell. No eye saw the bloody deed performed; no ear save your own caught the groans of your dying victims. You then and there robbed the living of life and then you robbed the dead of the reward of the honest toil which they had accumulated....

The judge continued:

For nine long years you have been a wanderer, upon the face of the earth, bowed and broken in spirit; no home, no loves, no ties to bind you to earth. You have been, indeed, a poor, pitiable waif of humanity. I hope and pray that in the spirit land to which you are so fast and surely drifting, you will find that peace and rest for your weary spirit which this world cannot give.

A stay of execution was granted to Packer on the grounds that the law under which he was found guilty was unconstitutional. During Packer's confinement in the Gunnison jail, while the courts were debating over his final fate, many people visited the cannibal. The jail became sort of a tourist attraction. Packer made hair watch chains from his shoulder length hair and curiosities from scraps of wood. He realized a good income from the tourists. His conviction was declared null and void due to a technicality in Colorado law between the time of the crime and his trial.

Packer was tried again in 1886, but this time for five counts of manslaughter. Again, he was found guilty and was sentenced to five consecutive terms of eight years each for his crimes. Finally in January 1901, Gov. Charles S. Thomas paroled him, but Governor Thomas reported later that Packer's letters to his relatives during his imprisonment were "...the foulest compositions I ever read and were filled with all sorts of threats against them in the event he regained his liberty."

The parole was granted due to Packer's poor health, but he was instructed to stay in Colorado. Governor Thomas commented many years later, "I don't know what became of him or when he died, but I am very sure that he was of no use to the community and probably a burden to himself."

Packer was found unconscious at the Cash Ranch in Deer Creek Canyon about 18 miles southwest of Englewood. He was suffering from epileptic fits and was taken to the home of the widow Van Alstine. He was cared for by the widow and her daughter, Mrs. Charles Cash. The two women stayed with the 64-year-old cannibal day and night. He finally began to talk, but it was always about his imprisonment for murders he said he did not commit. Packer related the tragedy of his life over and over again until the women grew indifferent to the story. For what he had done, he felt no church could give him absolution. He seemed to find no comfort in telling his story. He seemed to state it more as a puzzle that had no solution, and he continued to report his story over and over in a hopeless way.

Judge M. B. Gerry was supposed to have said to Alferd Packer when he was found guilty of murder and cannibalism, "Packer, ye man-eatin' son of a bitch, they was seven dimmycrats in Hinsdale County and ye eat five of 'em, God damn ye!" The statement actually came from a Lake City saloon keeper. (Colorado Historical Society)

As death approached, Mrs. Cash sat by Packer's bed and made the following observations:

> His face changed strangely before he died. It began to change Wednesday afternoon. A light came into it, and it looked like a field looks when the grass waves in the wind and the sun comes out from behind the clouds. He lay in bed all the afternoon smiling, smiling like a child that dreams in his sleep. And he never smiled much before.

53

Alferd Packer is buried in the Littleton cemetery. The name on his tombstone reads "Alfred Packer." Even after his death his first name was misspelled. The plateau above Lake City is now named Cannibal Plateau.

Professor James Starr headed a dig in July 1989, to add forensic evidence to the Packer story. At the burial site, the remains of his five companions were unearthed. Only four skulls were found, which agreed with the reports at the time of the burial. Of the five men, three showed signs that they tried to defend themselves based on multiple hatchet blows. Analysis indicated injuries made by a hatchet or machete on two of the skulls. All of the bones had been scraped clean with a knife supporting cannibalism. Starr and his team failed to find evidence that one of the men was shot, as Packer claimed. Only one old gunshot wound, that happened prior to the expedition, was discovered.

After 23 days of analysis in Tucson, the bones were returned for reburial. *Denver Post* reporter Kit Miniclier wrote

This plaque was placed near Lake City on what was later named Cannibal Plateau to mark the spot where the remains of Packer's five companions are buried. The plaque was erected in 1928 by the Ladies Union Aid Society of Lake City. (Kenneth Jessen)

that it was a gaudy event with the clergy dressed in black or dark gray and the 200 spectators in brightly colored clothing, shorts, sun glasses and sun hats. One of the four ministers selected the biblical verse, "It is written man does not live on bread alone," which brought laughter from the audience. The five victims were buried on the same spot but in a single coffin. The coffin was covered with a steel plate, and five metal crosses were placed in the ground above it.

### References
"A Cannibal's Confession." *Rocky Mountain News*, March 17, 1883.
"A Colorado Tragedy the Great Trial." *Gunnison Review Press*, August 4, 1886.
Bates, Margaret. *A Quick History of Lake City, Colorado*. Colorado Springs: Little London Press, pp. 14 17.
Bueler, Gladys R. *Colorado's Colorful Characters*. Boulder, Colorado: Pruett Publishing Co., 1981, pp. 60 61.
"Cannibalism dig finds no evidence Packer shot victim." *Loveland Reporter Herald*, August 5 6, 1989, p. 9.
"Change in venue." *Denver Tribune Republican*, July 23, 1886.
"*Denver Post* call for mercy and justice." *Denver Post*, January 8, 1900.
Eberhart, Perry. *Guide to the Colorado Ghost Towns and Mining Camps*. Denver: Sage Books, 1959, pp. 384 386.
Garner, Joe. "Packer victims reburied." *Rocky Mountain News*, August 15, 1989, p. 12.
"Governor Thomas tries to clear myth." *The Silver World*, November 29, 1930.
"Guilty to be hanged May 19, 1883." *Rocky Mountain News*, April 14, 1883.
"Human skull found one mile from scene." *Rocky Mountain News*, August 18, 1875.
Kushner, Ervan F. *Alferd G. Packer Cannibal! Victim?* Frederick, Colorado: Platte 'N Press, 1980.
"Man eater Packer captured." *Colorado Prospector*, Vol. 9, No. 2 (reprints of many articles relating to Alferd Packer).
"Man eater Packer captured." *Rocky Mountain News*, March 13, 1883.
"Man eater convicted." *Colorado Prospector*, Vol. 1, No. 2, p. 1 (reprints from the *Gunnison Review Press*, August 2, 1886, and August 5, 1886)
Miniclier, Kit. "No bones about it, Packer site reburial makes a gaudy event." *Denver Post*, August 15, 1989, p. 1A.
"Parole at Last." *Denver Post*, January 9, 1901.
Wright, Carolyn and Clarence Wright. *Tiny Hinsdale of the Silvery San Juan*. Big Mountain Press, 1964, pp 128 132.

# Prevaricator of Pikes Peak

The Signal Service (later named the Army Signal Corps) was designated to set up weather stations throughout the United States. The data proved valuable in understanding weather phenomena and led to the science of weather forecasting. In 1870, a station was constructed on top of 6,288-foot Mount Washington in New Hampshire. The Signal Service now looked to the Rocky Mountains for another mountaintop station. For a variety of reasons, including terrain and the location above the town of Colorado Springs, Pikes Peak was selected. Although only a primitive footpath led to the summit, it was one of the most accessible fourteeners in the state.

After construction difficulties at 14,110 feet, the Pikes Peak signal station was dedicated in October 1873. The barren summit provided plenty of rock for the structure, but all the lumber, telegraph poles, wire, batteries, tin sheets for the roof, stove, cooking utensils, furniture and so forth had to be brought by pack animals.

Collecting meteorological data was not the most interesting job, and the first news of something extraordinary appeared in the December 6, 1873, issue of the *Colorado Springs Weekly Gazette*. Sgt. Robert Seyboth reported that a monster lived in Mystic Lake, located just below timberline. As he was passing the lake one day on his trusty government mule, he heard a loud splashing sound. An animal of some sort, 100-feet long, was moving swiftly through the water. Its body was pale brown and covered with scales. Supported by its long, skinny neck, was a head with small eyes. Not content with the publicity from his first story, the sergeant told of meeting three Ute Indians on the trail. They said that the monster had lived in the lake for centuries and was especially fond of eating Utes, hav-

The U.S. Army Signal Corps weather station on the summit of Pikes Peak was a simple stone building. Several tons of rock were required to hold down the roof due to extreme windstorms. (Drawing by Kenneth Jessen)

ing devoured seven since last March. Seyboth's prevarication appeared in newspapers throughout the United States and in even a few papers in Europe.

Sergeant Seyboth had had enough. His bout with diphtheria combined with near frostbite of his fingers and toes put a great deal of strain on him resulting in loss of weight. After some turnover at the lofty signal station, Pvt. John Timothy O'Keeffe entered the scene. As far as a prevaricator, O'Keeffe raised the bar. The rather mundane temperature, wind velocity, rainfall and snowfall data must have stimulated O'Keeffe's creative juices, and he relished his visits to the saloons far below in Colorado City. He arrived January 5, 1875, and met Judge Eliphalet Price after an altercation in a bar. The two became friends and jointly concocted one of the most incredible stories every published.

In a co-authored story that appeared in the *Pueblo Chieftain* titled, "Attacked by rats, terrible conflict on the summit of Pikes Peak," May 25, 1876, O'Keeffe warned prospective visitors of a large number of vicious mountain rats. The rodents inhabited the rocky crevices on the summit of Pikes Peak and were aggressive and dangerous. O'Keeffe said that the rats normally fed on a saccharine gum that percolated through the pores of the rocks. The gum was freed from the rock by volcanic action that shook the mountain at irregular intervals.

The most noted characteristic of the rats, said O'Keeffe, was that they appeared only at night. During a full moon, he observed the rats swimming in a lake near the summit. They left a wake of sparkling light as they traversed the clear water.

One evening when O'Keeffe was hard at work in his office on his weather reports, he heard a scream from his wife. She ran into the room yelling, "The rats! The rats!" With great presence of mind, he immediately wrapped his wife in a sheet of zinc-plated steel. This protected her from the rats and prevented them from climbing on her. He quickly put stovepipes over his own legs. Using a heavy club, he fought the mountain rats as they entered through a window. The voracious rodents got into the kitchen and ate a quarter of beef in less than five minutes. This seemed to heighten their appetites. They viciously attacked Mrs. O'Keeffe, and despite the protective sheet of steel, some of the rodents managed to reach her face, leaving deep lacerations.

Right in the middle of this life-and-death struggle, Mrs. O'Keeffe grabbed a coil of wire hanging from the battery used for the telegraph system. She made spirals on the floor by tossing the coiled wire over to her husband. As the rats came in contact with the wire, they were electrocuted. The rats that survived were

Sergeant O'Keefe Brings Home the Game

O'Keeffe made his government mule, Balaam, into a legend of his own. In this illustration, Balaam is carrying O'Keeffe and a number of black-tailed deer. (From Rocky Mountain Tales)

driven back onto the barren, rocky summit of the mountain.

Tragically, the O'Keeffe's infant child, Erin, was eaten. Before the attack, Mrs. O'Keeffe had tried her best to protect the child by wrapping it in blankets. The mountain rats, however, had found their way to the infant girl lying helplessly in her crib, and all that remained was her small skull.

The story of the mountain rats and the O'Keeffe's tragic loss prompted more visitors to come to the summit and pay their respects. A cat named Erin was given to the private before he was assigned to the peak. O'Keeffe stood ready to sell photographs of his "baby" Erin to the tourists. On a pile of rocks, where a government burro was laid to rest, O'Keeffe erected a gravestone. It read, "Erected in Memory of Erin O'Keefe, daughter of John and Nora O'Keefe, who was eaten by mountain rats in the year 1876." (It should be noted that O'Keeffe also spelled his name O'Keefe.)

In the fall of 1876, O'Keeffe was relieved of his high-altitude duties and was sent through a training program. He was also promoted to sergeant. He returned to Pikes Peak in 1880. He had new story ideas, and in October, wrote a story titled, "Weather bound: wonderful adventures of a Signal Service officer on his way to the peak" that ran in the October 16, 1880, *Colorado Springs Gazette*.

In this story, Sergeant O'Keeffe went to Colorado Springs for supplies, and on the return trip, came across a large herd of black-tailed deer. He estimated there were 700 animals, so many that he had difficulty getting through the herd. O'Keeffe went on to report that it took an hour and 40 minutes for them to pass a given point!

Using his service revolver, he shot 17 animals for his meat supply at the weather station. He tied the tails of the deer together and slung them over the neck of his faithful government mule, Balaam. He and his mule continued up the steep trail until they passed timberline. They were stopped by a large snowdrift, and O'Keeffe cautiously made his way across it. At the other side, he

Sgt. John O'Keeffe erected this marker at the head of the grave of what he claimed was his little girl. According to a vivid account presented in local newspapers, O'Keeffe's child was eaten by mountain rats that attacked his family at the weather station on top of Pikes Peak.

looked for a route up the mountain. When O'Keeffe turned and looked back, Balaam had disappeared. The sergeant had survived the terrible raid by mountain rats and once again faced death, since all his provisions were on the back of his trusty mule.

After retracing his steps across the snowdrift, he tried to find Balaam and his supplies. The mule was in the bottom of a deep ravine and was lying with its feet in the air. It took O'Keeffe some time to recover the animal, the 17 deer and the supplies. Darkness was approaching, and it was too late to continue on to the summit. O'Keeffe and Balaam headed back to Colorado Springs. (Although highly exaggerated, this was based on an actual experience O'Keeffe had on one of his trips up the peak.)

On their way, they were ambushed by six hungry mountain lions. In order to escape, O'Keeffe was forced to toss the deer to the lions. Exhausted, the sergeant and his mule reached the safety of Colorado Springs at 8 p.m.

In the November 20, 1880, issue of the *Colorado Springs Gazette*, O'Keeffe reported that his safety was threatened by renewed volcanic activity on the mountain. During the night, the crater near the top of Pikes Peak began to discharge vapor. When O'Keeffe got close to investigate, the heat coming from the crater became oppressive and drove him back. There were signs of fresh ash and lava. The snow had melted back away from the edge of the crater.

While Sergeant O'Keeffe was making weather observations from the roof of the station, a violent eruption occurred. He reported to the newspapers that it was almost as spectacular as the one he witnessed at Mount Vesuvius in 1822. He was then just a boy, and it was before he decided to leave his native country of Italy. (O'Keeffe was Irish and was not born until well after 1822.)

Lava began pouring down Pikes Peak, and soon it was near Ruxton Creek. The residents of Colorado Springs became worried that the lava might reach the creek, turning its water into steam. O'Keeffe emphasized the serious nature of this event by pointing that this was the city's water supply. He speculated that if the eruption continued that Colorado Springs would meet the same fate as that which destroyed Pompeii and Herculaneum!

Sergeant O'Keeffe was quite proud of his 32-year-old government mule, Balaam. Balaam was the first mule to climb Pikes Peak. In fact, O'Keeffe claimed Balaam had made the trip 1,924 times, or an equivalent distance of 40,960 miles. Balaam also wore out 560 sets of shoes in the process.

At one time, Balaam was trapped on a rocky ridge, fighting three mountain lions. Whenever one of the lions would approach, Balaam would strike at it with his front feet, forcing it back. If a lion tried to attack from behind, Balaam would kick it in the ribs. The trio of lions did not give up until two of them were dead, their bodies lying at Balaam's feet.

These wonderful stories were the product of the imagination of John Timothy O'Keeffe, and they appeared in newspapers all over the United States. They provided comic relief to the drab, day-to-day life of an officer in the Signal Corps.

Just before Christmas 1881, Sergeant O'Keeffe resigned from the U.S. Army Signal Corps. Before he left the Colorado Springs area, he was given a banquet and was toasted as follows:

O'Keeffe, one of the greatest prevaricators, equaled by few, excelled by none. True to his record, may his life be a romance, and in his final resting place, may he lie easily. The first toast was followed by a second, The rosy realm of romance is as real to O'Keeffe as the stern and sterile steppes of truth are to many. The golden glow which gilds the granite summit of the peak is but the type of that glamour which surrounds it through the mendacious genius of O'Keeffe...Truth forever on the scaffold. Wrong forever on the throne...Gentlemen, here's looking at you.

O'Keeffe, in his own day, became a Colorado folk hero. At the age of 39, John O'Keeffe died suddenly. The *Rocky Mountain News* reported that, at the time of his death, he was a stoker on Steamer No. 2 for the Denver Fire Department's station on Colfax Avenue.

### References

Davidson, Levette Jay. "The Pikes Peak Prevaricator." *Colorado Magazine*, XX, No. 6 (November 1943), pp. 216 225.

Davidson, Levette Jay, and Forrester Blake, ed. *Rocky Mountain Tales*. Norman, Oklahoma: University of Oklahoma Press, 1947, pp. 227 256.

Hall, Frank. *History of Colorado*, Vol. III, Chicago: The Blakely Printing Company, 1895, pp. 374 376.

Rupp, Robert O. *Pikes Peak Duty*. Self published, 1987, pp. 55 58, p. 81.

Smith, Phyllis. *Weather Pioneers, the Signal Corps Station at Pikes Peak* Athens, Ohio: Ohio University Press, 1993, p. 5, pp. 58 67, 75 84.

The cure for tallow mouth was not without its side effects. It left its victims
bald. (Drawing by Kenneth Jessen)

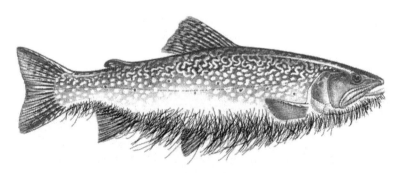

This is a *salvelinus fontinalis hairious,* a variant of the common brook
trout. It is found only in the headwaters of the Arkansas River and can be
caught using a barber pole. (Drawing by Kenneth Jessen)

# A Cure for Tallow Mouth

Some stories from the early days in Colorado were not only designed to entertain but to reflect on the difficulties of life. Living in Leadville could be miserable. Little medical care was available, and at an elevation of 10,152 feet above sea level, it was difficult to stay warm in drafty mining shanties. Tall tales originated under these adverse conditions and they were passed on to others as the absolute truth. For example, newcomers to Leadville were told that in 1877, meat became so scarce during the harsh winter that all the men could find to eat was venison and fried potatoes. They ate so much venison fat, or tallow, that it built up on the roofs of their mouths. This substantially cut down on conversation, and the miners only talked when it was essential. Eventually the tallow became so thick that the men couldn't even taste coffee or whiskey.

Many solutions were proposed and tried. According to the miners, the most effective was to cover the victim's head with pine knots and needles. Pine pitch was used to hold the mess together. Someone then set the heap on fire, and as the heat became intense, it melted the tallow from the roof of the miner's mouth and restored the victim's sense of taste. No cure such as this was entirely free of side effects, and in this case, the cure caused permanent baldness. By the end of the terrible winter of 1877, it was said that 97 percent of Leadville's miners were bald.

In the middle of the following spring, a gentleman from Kentucky reached Leadville and noticed the plight of the bald miners. He was in the hair tonic business and immediately began to manufacture his product from potatoes. Tallow mouth victims readily purchased his product.

One rainy summer evening, he was headed to town from his cabin with four jugs of hair tonic. He held on to one in each hand and tucked one under each arm. On the way, he was forced to cross a log over a small creek that emptied into the Arkansas River. He lost his balance momentarily on the slippery log and dropped the jugs under his arms. The two jugs broke when they hit the rocks in the stream.

Local fishermen downstream from the hair tonic maker's cabin reported that they switched fishing methods. Instead of using a rod and reel, they stuck a red, white and blue barber's pole in the bank, put on a white coat, waved a magazine in one hand and carried a pair of hair scissors in the other hand. When a fisherman called out "Next!" a fine hair-covered trout jumped out of the water to get a trim. In a short time, fishermen reached their limit using these tonsorial lures. This method of fishing continued until the mill tailings fouled the water so that the trout could no longer see the barber poles.

**References**

Blair, Edward. *Leadville: Colorado's Magic City.* Boulder: Pruett, 1980, p. 62.
Davidson, Levette Jay, and Forrester Blake, ed. *Rocky Mountain Tales.*
   Norman, Oklahoma: University of Oklahoma Press, 1947, pp. 258 259.
*Canon City Record*, February 16, 1939.

# The Solid Muldoon

Southern Colorado has always been a rich area for archaeologists, naturalists and geologists. Ancient pottery, tools and even human remains have been found there.

On September 20, 1877, William A. Conant traveled through the country southwest of Pueblo, and in the process, discovered a variety of fossils, including a sea turtle in an excellent state of preservation. He continued his search for more fossils and arrived in Pueblo with a large, stone figure of a man. His startling discovery made the headlines in practically every Rocky Mountain newspaper. The stone figure was found near the head of a long, dry arroyo about 25 miles from Pueblo. Conant related that he had to use a pick to free the figure from the hard clay. A cedar tree had extended its root between the arm and body of the figure, proving, said Conant, that it had been there for centuries.

Conant explained to the press that his discovery was made while he ate lunch. He spied a curious-looking stone protruding from the ground. Removing some of the loose clay, he found what resembled a human foot. At this point, he began to remove the clay to expose the entire figure. Unfortunately, in prying the figure from its grave, the head broke off at the neck.

Speculation was that the figure was the petrified body of a man, but others thought it was a piece of ancient sculpture because the figure seemed to be composed of a slate-like rock. It had a dirty yellow color, which was believed to be from its centuries of contact with the surrounding clay.

The statue was of a man in a reclining position with one arm crossed over the breast and the other lying along its side with the hand resting on the leg. The height of the giant was seven-and-a-half feet, and it weighed around 450 pounds.

Conant speculated on what type of human race the body represented. The face had Asiatic features with high cheekbones. The figure was thin, much like men in ancient Egyptian pictures. The most remarkable feature of all was a tail about two inches long at the end of the backbone. The arms were ape-like in appearance and, if straightened, would reach below the knee. The feet were long and flat. The big toe was a full two inches shorter than the middle toes. Newspapermen added that this creature was strongly suggestive of the truth of the Darwinian Theory and could very well be the "missing link" between man and ape.

Upon examination by experts, there appeared to be no doubt that the figure was genuine. The stone showed all the effects of time, and the circumstances of the discovery seemed to fit into place.

The Colorado giant was dubbed the "Solid Muldoon" and became the chief topic of the day. It was said to be one of the new wonders of the world, and people from all over the United States came to examine it in a Pueblo theater.

E. Shelburne, editor of the *Pueblo Colorado Weekly Chieftain*, was skeptical, especially after a visit by Phineas Taylor Barnum to see the Solid Muldoon. Barnum was well established in exploiting his fellow man. To say the least, he was an accurate judge of American susceptibility to suggestion. Shelburne set out with three other men to visit the would-be discovery site. The location was halfway up a small hill. (This hill was later named Muldoon Hill and is located along Colorado Highway 78.) The earth was composed of shale right down to the bottom of the excavation. A sign had been left behind by Conant which read, "This mount is given the name of Ancient Mount, named by W. A. Conant. A petrified man or beast was found here by me."

The men, under the direction of the editor, looked at the bottom of the excavation for some indentation produced by the long repose of the solid stony form. They were unable to discover any hint that the Solid Muldoon had ever been there. As

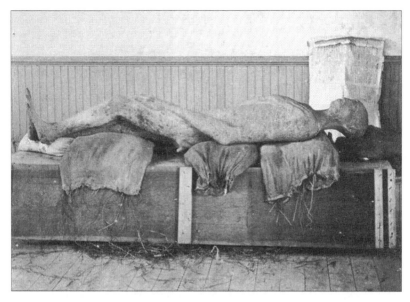

One of the West's greatest hoaxes was the Solid Muldoon. It was "discov-ered" near Pueblo and was passed off as a petrified man. It measured more than seven feet in height and was cast out of Portland cement.
(Denver Public Library, Western History Department)

for the root that supposedly had grown between the arm and the body, the largest root that entered the excavation measured no more than threeeighths of an inch across.

Shelburne smelled a rat and concluded, "It would be almost as much impossible for that stony form to lay imbedded in the earth and leave no impression as it would be for a tree to make no shade when the sun was shining on it. In fact, the whole thing is too thin, and smells of P. T. Barnum."

A reporter from the *Kansas City Times* interviewed Barnum regarding Conant's find. It is interesting to note how little informa-tion was obtained in the interview. The reporter began by asking,

> Mr. Barnum, is the Pueblo Petrification a real, solid, bona fide stone man, or is it another Cardiff Giant (a hoax per-petrated in 1869)?

Barnum:
I believe it to be just what it is represented to be. If I had not, I would not have offered Mr. Conant $20,000 for it.

Reporter:
Did you really offer the owner that amount of money for it?

Barnum:
I did, and he refused it, but he offered to sell me threefourths and retain onefourth interest in it.

Reporter:
So you feel assured, Mr. Barnum, that this new discovery is what it is claimed to be — a real petrified man?

Barnum:
No. I won't say that it is a petrified man, but either man or beast petrified into stone. I feel sure of this, because in the excavation or resurrection of the stone corpse, the head broke from the shoulders and there was a weathered, crystallized spine and other bones as natural as life. Oh, no, sir, I am sure that this is no Cardiff Giant affair.

Reporter:
How does it look?

Barnum:
Well, sir, it is a well-defined human body petrified into solid stone. The most singular part of it is its tail, which is well defined and an unmistakable part of the body....

Reporter:
Perhaps it is a petrified gorilla, Mr. Barnum?

Barnum:
No, no, I do not think so. The cheek bones are high and projecting, like the American Indian, and the formation of hands and feet indicate that it is not of the monkey species.

The reporter grew more excited as Barnum added the icing to the cake.

Reporter:
What do you think it is?

Barnum:
Well, sir, it is my candid opinion that in this discovery we have found the missing link which Darwin claims connects mankind with the beast creation. It is certainly the petrified body of a man with a tail, and was dug up by an old man named W. A. Conant near Pueblo.

Reporter:
Is he a reliable party, Mr. Barnum? Perhaps it is a put-up job on you and the public.

Barnum:
Yes, he is reliable. He is a respectable old man and is an agent for the Atchison, Topeka & Santa Fe Railroad. He was once a member of the New York legislature, and is much respected in Colorado where he had lived for several years. He says he will not sell the petrification until it has been examined by Professor Marsh (a prominent anthropologist of the day) or some other authority.

P. T. Barnum continued his journey back to his palatial home in Bridgeport, Connecticut.

On October 25, 1877, the *Pueblo Colorado Weekly Chieftain* decided to publish the opinion of Professor John L. Boggs, a noted phrenologist, who lived about seven or eight miles from the site of the find. Boggs, a resident of the territory for 17 years, was considered to have sound judgment. The colorful report by Boggs reads, in part, as follows:

Will you please give me space...to give the public a few graphic ideas in reference to that gigantic and formidable man, specter, apparition, ghost, or image, that was exhumed in Colorado on September 20, 1877, by Mr. Conant of Colorado Springs, measuring seven feet eight inches in height said form being nearly perfect except for a rent diagonally across the sternum, exposing some of the respiring [sic] organs? Yes, some people a little more imaginary, say they saw him breathe as he lay on his couch in Pueblo, in the old theatre building. So perfect were his smiles of congratulation that the over spiritual on entering the room would almost say, 'Howdy, Mr. Petrified Indian.'...I have visited the tomb in person, and Dr. Shelburne, Mr. Struile, Mr. Laking, and others from Pueblo have also paid a visit lately to the mound of ancient idols and of the heathen aborigine...And in all examinations yet made around the giant's grave not a piece of ancient armor had ever been found, such as a scepter, crown, shield, lance, spear, bow, quiver, gun, butcher knife, nor tomahawk. Such armor, all or in part, would surely have been used by this giant king of the Lamonites ...or more modern aborigines, who seldom ever bury their dead without them.

But this body was not well proportioned, for the three lower vertebrae protrude, and the...hand reached clear below the scapula joints, and the matter is in great doubt whether this is not similar to some objects of sculptured work in stone to be found in modern times by the antiquarian along the Nile in the form of the Sphinx...You will please allow me to differ from scientists if they should pronounce him a real petrified Indian of the Rocky Mountains.

But it is no different whether an idol, image, or rock, is surely a magnificent humbug for Barnum.

Your title, race, or blood,

Say, did you live before or since the flood?

It was a mighty blunder, When this statue fell asunder.

(signed)   Prof. Boggs

Mr. Fitch was the proprietor of a factory for manufacturing artificial stone using what was known as the "Rollins carbureted stone process." His plant was located in the northern part of Connecticut.

Mr. Hull, the very same individual who sculptured the magnificent 10-foot Cardiff Giant in 1869, contacted Fitch in February 1876. After the two men talked for a while, Hull offered Fitch money to aid in the creation of what he referred to as a "new curiosity." Hull's Cardiff Giant had been exposed as a hoax in 1870, and now he was ready to tackle a new project. He told Fitch he wanted to get some bones cast into the figure for authenticity but did not know how. Fitch said he could manage it.

A secret plant was set up in an icehouse leased by Hull on a farm in Pennsylvania. Hull began by making molds for the petrified man while Fitch did the casting. The molds of the lower portion of the body were taken from Hull's son-in-law.

He was a slender young fellow over six feet tall with long legs and arms. Sections of approximately a foot in length were molded by Hull, and immediately filled with Portland cement by Fitch. The marks where the sections joined were clearly visible. Fitch could not conceive of how these people apparently failed to notice them.

Every time another segment was cast, Hull's son-in-law had to strip. The icehouse was very chilly, and the model constantly complained, then finally walked off the job. Hull had to use his own body to make the casts of the upper portion of the figure. Hull's build, however, was the exact opposite of his son-in-law's. Hull was short, thickset, and had a large chest. This, of course, accounted for the disproportion of the figure and thus accidentally added to its mystery.

The statue was built in an erect position using Portland cement mixed with brown pigment. After a molded section was completed, it would be placed into position and stuffed with cement.

A human skeleton was purchased, and portions of it were utilized in various parts of the statue where examinations would likely be made by scientists. Bones were placed all the way up both legs, and a straight bone was stuck in the lower portion of the back with an inch protruding to keep the tail from breaking off. To strengthen the upper part of the body, the shinbone from a cow was inserted through the neck from the middle of the head down to the center of the chest. A piece of skull was placed in back of the left ear, where later the statue was bored to prove its authenticity. In case scientists looked for a backbone, some ground bones were moistened, rolled into little lumps, and placed down the middle of the back.

The completed figure was laid on a brick platform above a furnace. Over the platform was a tent-like structure. Fitch burned charcoal to make carbonic acid gas. The gas was trapped by the tent-like structure and surrounded the figure. The gas acted on the moist cement and turned it into a stone-like material after about a week. At the time, this process was little known by scientists. The cement used to create the Solid Muldoon cost only $11.45.

Despite this economy, Hull used all of his money, about $6,000 during the construction of the statue. He contacted P. T. Barnum to see if he would be interested in investing in the hoax. Barnum sent an agent to examine the statue. The agent's report was satisfactory, and Barnum purchased part interest in it. After all, it was Barnum's motto that "…a sucker is born every minute."

The statue was shipped to Colorado Springs in a machinery crate. W. A. Conant, an employee of Barnum, received the shipment and arranged to have it transported out into the countryside near Pueblo to be "discovered." Barnum made sure he was in Colorado shortly after the discovery to play the role of an interested investor.

A pair of noted professors was hired by Barnum to examine the statue and make a report. They had no idea they were part of a scam. Hull traveled from Connecticut to assist the professors and listened carefully to what tests they would make. He learned that if the Solid Muldoon were truly a petrified man, calcite crystals would likely be found in its interior. Hull volunteered to do the boring and, without being observed, carefully held some calcite crystals between his thumb and forefinger. He slowly introduced the crystals into the material that came from the statue. The learned men were hoodwinked. After its stay in Pueblo, Barnum arranged to have the Solid Muldoon transported to the New York Museum of Anatomy. This museum was owned by Barnum, and more scientists were allowed to examine it. This time, they demanded that a second bore be made into the stomach area. Hull was kept busy at night chiseling a hole into the stomach, then inserting a number of calcite crystals. The hole was then covered with some colored Portland cement and hardened. But Fitch couldn't stand the burden of secrecy, and just before the scientists were going to cross-section the stomach area, he exposed the hoax.

**References**
"Careful construction for a hoax is told." *New York Times*, February 7, 1878.
"Petrified man discovered near Beulah." *Pueblo Colorado Weekly Chieftain*, September 20, 1877.
"Prof. Boggs comments on muldoon." *Pueblo Colorado Weekly Chieftain*, October 25, 1877.
"P. T. Barnum hits town!" *Pueblo Daily Chieftain*, September 22, 1877.
"P. T. Barnum offers to purchase muldoon." *Pueblo Daily Chieftain*, September 29, 1877.
"Sweet land of promise     Beulah." *Colorado Prospector*, Vol. 12, No. 8, p. 1 (originally published on February 6, 1877, in the *Pueblo Daily Chieftain*).
"The Colorado giant, the Solid Muldoon." *Pueblo Colorado Weekly Chieftain*, September 27, 1877.
Uchill, Ida Libert. *Howdy, Sucker! What P. T. Barnum Did in Colorado*. Denver: Pioneer Peddler Press, 2001, pp. 77 86.
Wyant, Walter. *The Colorado Giant*. Pueblo, Colorado: Beulah Historical Society, 1980.

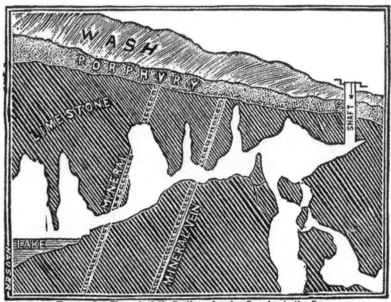

FIGURE 1.—Characteristic Section, showing Opening to the Cave.

This drawing appeared in *Crofutt's Guide to Colorado* and depicts Orth Stein's imaginary Cyclopean Cave. Stein wrote articles about fictitious places, but he added almost believable realism by using actual geographical features and the names of people known to his readers.

(Denver Public Library, Western History Department)

# Underground Fantasies

In 1878, only a few hundred miners were working in the Leadville area, and after large silver strikes, the population jumped to an estimated 30,000. By 1880, Leadville was alive with excitement. Prosperity from the rich mines fueled the town's aroundtheclock, carnivallike atmosphere.

A small man dressed in a typical eastern-cut suit stepped off the early morning Denver & Rio Grande train at the Leadville depot. His name was Orth Stein, and his starched collar and derby hat set him apart from the casual dress of the hundreds of people that filled Leadville's streets. Smoke from belching smelters blackened the sky, and ore wagons jammed the roads down from the mines. The wheels of heavily loaded ore wagons ground the unpaved streets into a quagmire of mud. Leadville was a rip-roaring town with 82 saloons, 21 gambling establishments, 35 houses of prostitution, 38 restaurants, four theaters and three newspapers. Not all of the many who worked in the mines could find lodging and slept on the filthy, sawdust-covered floors in the numerous saloons.

Stein was a perceptive journalist hired by Carlyle C. Davis, publisher of the *Leadville Chronicle*. Leadville was unbelievable in its violence, shootings and bizarre behavior, but Stein would surpass that reality with his own brand of imaginative fantasies.

Stein wasn't expected to show up at the *Chronicle* office until evening, so he set out to do some sightseeing. He pushed his way through the crowds moving along Chestnut Street. As he passed down the busy street, he noticed an unusual number of doctor's offices. Curiosity prompted him to visit a few of them.

He pretended to be a medical student, and his eastern outfit made his story believable. He told the various "doctors" that he was in Leadville for some practical experience, noting that their credentials hung unusually high on their office walls. At one office, Stein removed a "diploma" from its frame while the doctor was out of the room. It was nothing more than a certificate from a plasterers' union. As he traveled around Leadville, he encountered other "doctors" who boasted of their high fees and how they practiced without any education in medicine.

By late afternoon, Stein had sufficient evidence for a great exposé. He wrote the story, went to the *Chronicle* office and introduced himself to his employer, Carlyle Davis. To the amazement of the publisher, who was about to give Stein his first assignment, the new reporter turned over the completed manuscript. Davis was so impressed that he promoted Stein from cub reporter to city editor on the spot. The next day, the *Chronicle* ran an exposé on how few of Leadville's doctors were legitimate.

Given a pad of paper, Orth Stein could excite, infuriate and insult his readers. His reporting was excellent, but this was not what made him famous. Stein generated some of the greatest tongueincheek tales ever to appear in the West.

For example, in one of his articles, Stein imagined himself walking over the mountains one Sunday afternoon. He stepped on a soggy area that suddenly gave way. After slipping some distance down a 45-degree slope, he found himself in a vast cavern with arched entrances leading into it from all sides. Connected to the cavern through these openings were many vaulted chambers.

A stream ran through the main cavern, which also contained a great deal of placer gold. Stein was not alone. Several miners were busy panning the precious metal. Exposed veins of rich ore could be seen on the cavern walls. Having not been observed, Stein tried to slip away unnoticed. He planned to stake his own claim to this rich underground property. He couldn't get back up the steep incline, however, and was forced to reveal himself to the miners. Only after Stein agreed to file a claim on behalf of the miners did they agree to show him how to get out of the cavern.

Stein was a genius of the editorial hoax. To bring credibility to his stories, he used the names of real people, actual geographical features and laced them with elaborate details. He also serialized his fantasies. The article about the cavern and the miners set the stage for a sequel published in September 1882.

The cavern was further explored. It had great dome ceilings, stalactites and mineralization in its walls. The side chambers were given names like Chronicle Rotunda, Bridal Veil, Serpent's Glen and Stein Gallery. It was the kind of rich, subterranean cavern that all miners and prospectors dreamed they could find. And naturally, Stein didn't keep the place secret. In one of his imaginative articles, he "invited" 50 well-known Leadville residents to explore the cavern with him. He named it Cyclopean Cave, and as other stories appeared, new "discoveries" were made.

An underground lake was added, and Stein described it as follows:

> No current seems to disturb its placid surface; no living thing finds life within its depths; all is silent as the grave within this buried pool, where never yet a breeze had stirred a ripple or a sunbeam played...All of the lake is not visible from any one spot. In fact, it loses itself beneath a low rocky arch into the inky darkness beyond.

Stein carried his description of Stein Gallery further into the abstract by likening it to the Vatican by moonlight. Its ceiling was fringed with white, sparkling stalactites. With little modesty, he concluded, "This apartment had been named in honor of a Leadville newspaper man."

So believable was the Cyclopean Cave, George Croffut listed it in his *Grip-Sack Guide to Colorado*. Drawings of the cave were included.

As Christmas 1882 approached, Stein was in rare form when he related a story about a particular mine. After giving it a perfectly believable location, he continued to tell how a miner struck a hard boulder imbedded in a soft limestone formation. In the boulder was a perfectly formed shoe. It appeared to be made of old, mildewed leather, but when the miner touched it, the shoe turned out to be composed of stone. The miner believed it to be a petrified shoe from some ancient time. Every detail had been preserved, including a repair made to the shoe. Possibly to test the gullibility of his readers, Stein wrote that the stone shoe was on display at Livezey's Fifth National Loan office in the Clarendon Hotel block. He advised his readers not to miss it. It is unknown how many went to see the fictitious shoe, nor how the management of the loan office explained that they did not have such a shoe.

Of all Stein's stories, one of the most farfetched involved a sailing ship stranded in a giant cavern 50 feet underground. He began the story with a pair of prospectors who were sinking a shaft in a desolate area near Leadville. At the depth of 15 feet, they heard a hollow sound each time their picks struck the bottom of the shaft. The clever prospectors tied themselves with ropes and continued digging. The bottom of the shaft finally fell away leaving the men dangling by their ropes. They gazed into a room 240 feet by 180 feet. The prospectors managed to reach a ledge and then a natural stairway.

In Stein's own words:

> Down this they scrambled, impelled by curiosity and a spirit of adventure, holding their miner's lamps above their heads and soon stood upon a tolerably level sanded floor with here and there a huge crystal of quartz, while from the roof, which arched overhead at a distance of about fifty feet, enormous stalactites [were] suspended like icicles, and catching the feeble rays of light, threw them back in a myriad of rainbow hues. The cave seemed at first empty, but as their eyes gradually became accus-

tomed to the deep gloom, the men saw in a further extremity a huge black object, which, not without some trepidation, they approached.

As they neared it, to their unbounded amazement, they made out the outlines of some sort of sailing craft, but the idea of a ship fifty feet underground was so preposterous that they thought it some fantastic mess of rocks, and not until they fairly touched the timbers would they believe the evidence of their own senses. A ship it plainly was or had been, but a ship different from any that the eyes of the astonished miners had ever looked upon. It was, as nearly as they could judge, about sixty feet long by some thirty feet wide, and lay tilted forward at an angle about fifteen degrees over a rough pile of stone. The body of the craft was built of short lengths of some dark and very porous wood, resembling our black walnut, if it could be imagined, with the grain pulled apart like a sponge or a piece of bread, and made perfectly square.

Both ends (it was evidently intended for sailing either way) were turned up like the toe of a peaked Moorish slipper. The planking was apparently double-riveted with nails of extremely hard copper, only slightly rust-eaten, and with the heads cut or filed in an octagonal shape, while along the upper edge of the ship eleven large rings of the same metal and evidently for the securing of rigging....

Stein continued his detailed story of the subterranean ship, making it grow in the minds of his readers. The story ended as follows:

The discovery of the junk-like ship with its unknown architecture, hermetically sealed in a cavern fifty feet below the surface of the earth, gives scope to infinite speculation. The only possible explanation seems, however, that in ages ago...a vessel bearing a crew of bold discoverers, tossed by the waves then receding, left it stranded there and the great continental divide, the awful upheavals and convulsions of nature, which were known so little of and can only blindly speculate on, pressed the face of the earth together and sealed it in a living grave. And this is but a groping guess, yet in what strange old seas the vessel sailed, what unknown, ancient waters pressed against its peaked prow, under what pre-historic skies it pitched, what man can tell?

The fine detail in this story gives it certain validity. Stein's fantasies didn't hurt the *Chronicle's* circulation either. Publisher C. C. Davis allowed Stein to diverge from his normal reporting duties to write another story. After a while, the newspaper readers didn't take any of Stein's stories seriously, and his stories became a source of amusement.

It must not be overlooked that Stein was also a great reporter with a natural nose for news. But it was difficult at times to separate fact from fiction. Soon after President James A. Garfield's assassination, a quiet little woman entered the newspaper office. She purchased back issues of the *Chronicle* published since the assassination. She explained that she had been in the mountains and wanted to catch up on the news. Only Stein seemed interested in her, and he followed her home. He questioned her and discovered she was Mrs. Guiteau, the ex-wife of the president's assassin. She showed Stein letters written by her former husband that shed new light on the events leading to Garfield's untimely end. This information was used to produce a powerful story, which ran in July 1881. The story was of national interest and was reprinted in newspapers all over the United States. It later turned out that Mrs. Guiteau existed only in the mind of Orth Stein.

The *Chronicle* should have been only a stepping-stone in a great writing career for Orth Stein. Instead, it was the beginning and the end. Stein left Leadville in 1882 and was almost beaten to death near a Denver hotel. He never fully recovered from his injuries. He changed his name to John Bell and moved to Kansas City. He became infatuated with a young woman who happened to be the mistress of the owner of a hotel and theater, George Fredricks. Stein would sneak into Fredricks room to be with the young lady while Fredricks was tending to his duties at the theater. Eventually, Stein was caught in the act, but Fredricks did little. After getting caught several times, Fredricks started beating the young woman. Stein let his .44 caliber revolver speak by shooting Fredricks in the head, killing him. Stein's mother spent a small fortune in his defense to save him from prison. After an extended illness, Stein died in 1901.

### References

Blair, Edward. *Everybody Came to Leadville*. Leadville, Colorado: Timberline Books, 1971, pp. 20 23.

Bower, Donald E. "The fantastic world of Orth Stein." *American West*, May 1973, pp. 13 16, 61 63.

Griswold, Don L., and Jean Harvey Griswold. *History of Leadville and Lake County, Colorado*. Denver: Colorado Historical Society, 1996, pp. 666 667, 1171 1175.

Parris, Lloyd E. *Caves of Colorado*. Boulder, Colorado: Pruett Publishing Co., 1973, pp. 42 51.

# Bosco's Baggage

The narrow-gauge Rio Grande Southern served many Colorado mining towns, including Placerville, Telluride, Durango, Ridgway and Rico. Telluride was reached by a branch of the Rio Grande Southern that left the main line at Vance Junction. About a half-mile away lived Colonel Vance. He was a bachelor who stayed in a small cabin and was periodically drunk. He would go on a binge every payday.

On one particular day, Col. James Vance came to the depot at Vance Junction following a serious drinking bout. After a brief visit, he ventured up the lush hillside catching big, green grasshoppers.

A snake charmer named Bosco had finished his show at Telluride and was on his way south to give another show at Rico. He had to transfer from the local Telluride train to the southbound train and was forced to wait at Vance Junction. He entered the depot with a suitcase full of snakes, but when his train arrived, Conductor Sanders would not allow the snakes on board. Bosco had to leave the suitcase in the office to be forwarded on the next southbound freight.

In the meantime, the Colonel was still on the hill above the depot catching grasshoppers when the depot agent called to him to come down. The agent wanted to surprise the Colonel with the contents of the suitcase. The Colonel was so hung over that when he saw the snakes, he wasn't afraid and grabbed an armful of the serpents. The astonished agent watched as the Colonel scattered them all over the office area. Included were rattlers, water snakes and dozens more. The agent spent the day sweeping snakes out of the Vance Junction depot. After the Colonel sobered up a little, it became clear to him what he had done, and he became scared stiff.

Vance Junction sat up on the side of a hill. This is how it looked after the abandonment of the Rio Grande Southern.
(Denver Public Library, Western History Department)

This unfortunate incident put Bosco temporarily out of business. He cursed the conductor when he learned what had happened to his "performers." He returned to Vance Junction to salvage what he could, but some of the snakes already had gone off into the woods.

### References

Collman, Russ, Dell A. McCoy, and William A. Graves. *The R.G.S. Story*, Vol. III. Denver: Sundance Publications Ltd., 1993, p. 14.

Crum, Jose Moore. *The Rio Grande Southern Railroad*. Durango: San Juan History, Inc., 1961, (taken from "Snakes in the Depot" by John Houk), p. 288.

Eldon Ashbaugh standing on the partially completed rock wall constructed by the Denver, South Park & Pacific. (Kenneth Jessen)

# The Great Rock Wall

High on the mountainside near the gravel road leading up Ohio Creek north of Gunnison stands a large rock wall. It sits on a steep talus slope and spans the gap between two cliffs. Upon close examination, it is apparent that the wall was never completed as evidenced by the large steps along its top. About eight-feet thick, the wall is composed of hand-fitted rock laid without mortar. The wall stands about 45-feet above its base, and if it had been completed, it would have been 60-feet high.

At either end of the wall are shelves cut into the cliffs that form a constant grade headed toward Ohio Pass. Downgrade and away from the pass, the grade ends abruptly in an aspen grove at the edge of another talus slope. Piles of rock, however, mark what would have been the route across the slide. By connecting completed portions of the grade, it is apparent that the jeep road directly below the wall is part of a giant loop used to reverse direction and gain altitude.

The great wall is part of a railroad grade and represents the last attempt by the narrow-gauge Denver, South Park & Pacific to reach westward into Utah. The wall is a tribute to the tenacity of its builders, yet it is a monument to the failure of the railroad to attain its goal. It stands above conifer forests and rich meadows filled with wild flowers to remind us of ambitious times during the 1880s to develop the state's resources.

The Denver, South Park & Pacific began construction in Denver in 1873, and reached Morrison the following year. From this humble beginning, the railroad grew to become Colorado's largest narrow-gauge system with 335 miles of track. It headed south out of Denver, west through Platte River Canyon and over Kenosha Pass. It crossed South Park through Fairplay and, via Trout Creek Pass, reached Buena Vista in the Arkansas

**The great rock wall as seen from the Ohio Pass road is quite imposing.**
(Kenneth Jessen)

River Valley. From there, it went up Chalk Creek Canyon through the mining town of St. Elmo, then through the Alpine Tunnel at an elevation of 11,523 feet. From there, the line dropped down Quartz Creek through Pitkin to Gunnison.

The Denver, South Park & Pacific reached Gunnison in 1882, and the railroad announced plans to continue construction to the west. Grading began up Ohio Creek in January 1882,

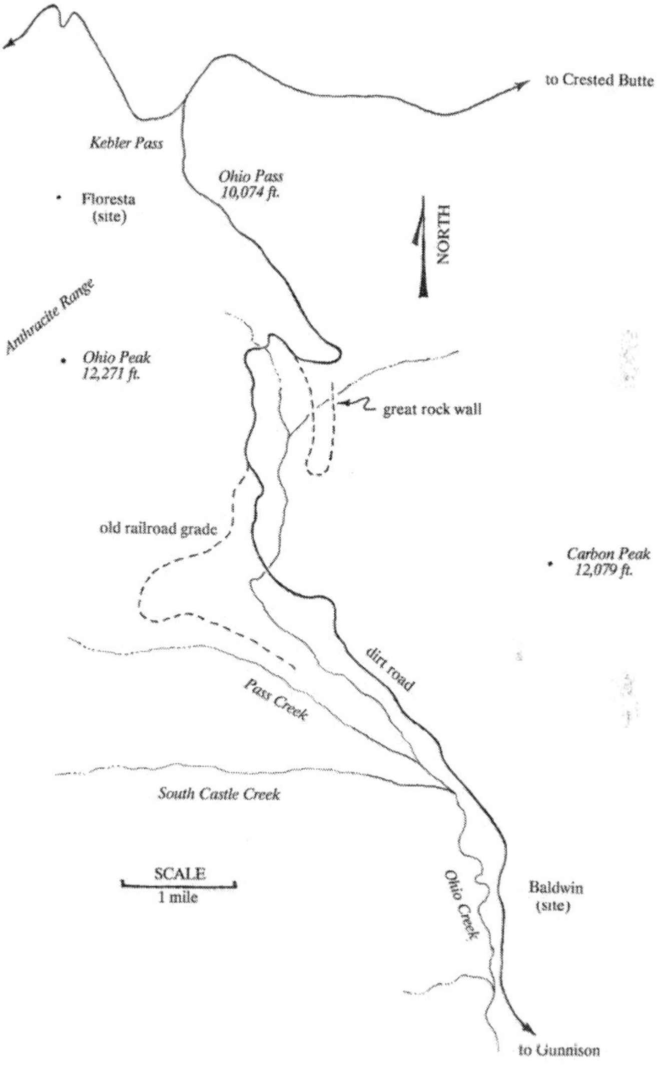
to Crested Butte
Kebler Pass
Ohio Pass
10,074 ft.
Floresta
(site)
NORTH
Anthracite Range
Ohio Peak
12,271 ft.
great rock wall
old railroad grade
Carbon Peak
12,079 ft.
dirt road
Pass Creek
South Castle Creek
SCALE
1 mile
Ohio Creek
Baldwin
(site)
to Gunnison

**The Great Rock Wall is south of Ohio Pass in Gunnison County and can be seen from a graded dirt road.** (Map drawn by Kenneth Jessen)

with plans to go over Ohio Pass and down Anthracite Creek on the west side of Kebler Pass. The great rock wall was built during the spring. The following year the rails reached Castleton, 15 miles north of Gunnison. The line was extended another three miles to serve the New Baldwin Mine. This coal mine was as close as the Denver, South Park & Pacific trains came to the Utah state line.

In 1883, the Denver, South Park & Pacific abandoned its construction up Ohio Creek in favor of an easier grade via the Gunnison River and Slate Creek to Crested Butte. This route paralleled its rival, the narrow-gauge Denver & Rio Grande. It was to pass through Crested Butte, but no grading was ever completed.

The cave-in of the Alpine Tunnel closed the Denver, South Park & Pacific's route to Gunnison in 1888. The tunnel was reopened in 1895, but because of operating expenses associated with the high altitude and heavy winter snow, the tunnel was closed permanently in 1910. The Denver, South Park & Pacific turned over the operation of its spurs north of Gunnison to the Denver & Rio Grande. The last train puffed up Ohio Creek to the New Baldwin Mine in 1952, and two years later the track was removed.

The railroad grades of the Denver, South Park & Pacific and the Denver & Rio Grande are now overgrown with vegetation. Ties have long rotted away leaving only a trail of cinders. The trestles were removed, but a few water tanks and depots remain. The one enduring durable feature, however, is the great rock wall of Ohio Creek.

References

Hauck, Cornelius W. "The South Park Line, A Concise History." *Colorado Rail Annual No. 12*. Golden: Colorado Railroad Museum, 1974, pp. 150, 151, 190.

Ormes, Robert. *Tracking Ghost Railroads in Colorado*. Colorado Springs: Century One Press, 1975, p. 70.

Poor, Mac C. *Denver South Park & Pacific*. Denver: Rocky Mountain Railroad Club, 1976, pp. 232 235.

# Pigg Hunts Bear

The legend of Old Mose began in the fall of 1883, when Jacob Radliff traveled 45 miles from his home in Fairplay to the Black Mountain area to hunt deer and elk. Meat of this type was a staple for the miners, and the game in the Fairplay area had been depleted. Miners were willing to pay in gold for fresh meat, and this motivated Radliff and his companions.

On their third day of hunting, the men split up. While crossing a small meadow, Radliff saw the tracks of a huge bear. He was not interested in hunting bear and continued across the meadow. As he reached the timber on the opposite side, an enormous grizzly bear came out of the underbrush directly toward him. Radliff got off one quick shot before the bear hit him and broke the bones in one ankle. The bear grabbed Radliff and bit both of his legs, snapping the bones like sticks. The bear used his claws to slash open Radliff's face and back. The bear seemed infuriated by Radliff's screams and tossed the man into the air. Finally, the bear tore off Radliff's scalp.

One of Radliff's hunting companions heard the shot and the screams. He ran to help but when he arrived the bear was gone, and the badly injured Radliff was barely conscious. Horrified, he ran and got Radliff's other companion, and the two men placed the injured man on a litter. They carried him back to camp and put him in a wagon. After the horses were hitched, they traveled as fast as they could down the mountain. The jolting on the rough road brought more agony to Radliff as he continued to lose blood.

It was dark when they reached the nearest ranch owned by the Mulock family. Radliff's bleeding was so great that blood dripped from the bottom of the wagon box. The injured man was carefully carried inside where Mrs. Parker Mulock tried to

The *Denver Post* ran this story about the killing of Old Mose in its Sunday edition on May 15, 1904. (Kenneth Jessen Collection)

help him. She also put the poor man's scalp back in place. A cowboy named Hyssong immediately rode for eight hours in the dark to the nearest railroad station on the Denver, South Park & Pacific. Here he telegraphed Fairplay for a doctor. Around 8 a.m., the doctor arrived by special train and began the long ride back to the Mulock ranch with Hyssong.

In the meantime, Radliff suffered through the night but did regain consciousness long enough to tell those around him about the large bear. When he finished, he looked his companions in the eye and said, "Boys, don't hunt that bear." A short time later Jacob Radliff died. Hyssong and the doctor arrived too late. After a well attended funeral, Jacob Radliff was buried in the Fairplay cemetery.

News of Radliff's death at the hands of a vicious bear became the topic of conversation for months to come. Brave men (after a few drinks) swore to hunt down and kill the bear to avenge Radliff's death. As winter wore on, the bear was soon forgotten by all except for one individual.

At the small community of Currant Creek, a Pigg became interested in hunting the bear. This was Wharton Pigg, who knew that the bear was now in hibernation for the winter of 1883-1884. When spring arrived, Pigg began hunting in the Black Mountain area. He methodically used a map to mark the location where ranchers reported seeing bear tracks or, in some cases, having their cattle slaughtered. After two years, Pigg concluded that the big bear had a range of 600 square miles, but for all his efforts, he never sighted a bear of any kind.

Because the tracks of the big grizzly seemed to mosey around randomly with no particular route, the bear became known as Old Mose. Ranchers continued to report big bear tracks and loss of cattle. Some even claimed to have gotten off a shot or two at the animal.

Eventually, Pigg was successful at killing a sow and her cub. In October 1894, he received some disturbing news that Old Mose had been killed on Thirty-Five Mile Mountain by a local rancher who had spent the previous three days hunting the animal. The bear's weight was nearly a half ton, and its carcass filled a wagon box. This was bad news for Pigg, who remained depressed all winter.

The following spring, Pigg found big footprints once again near Black Mountain. Old Mose was alive, and all summer long, Pigg hunted the bear. At times, the tracks seemed only minutes old and he knew he was hot on the trail of Old Mose.

Pigg discovered gold ore near Cripple Creek and worked the mine to raise money. He realized, however, that he couldn't mine and hunt Old Mose at the same time. When he sold his mine in 1896, he was wealthy enough to hunt Old Mose full time through the forests, meadows and trails near Black Mountain. Eventually, Pigg purchased the 56,000 acre Stirrup Ranch on the east side of Black Mountain. It was filled with game and was a hunter's paradise. The ranch house was only six miles from where Jacob Radliff had been attacked.

At Fairplay, cattlemen built a substantial trap: a pen with three-foot walls. On one side, there was a gap in the wall. A dead cow was placed in the pen, and a bear trap was concealed at the entrance. Old Mose robbed this pen three times by reaching over the wall and lifting the heavy carcass out.

A horse killed by lightning on the Dave Walker ranch was left in a pasture surrounded by a stake fence. Every night, Old Mose went into the pasture for a feast. Each time, however, the bear selected a new route, knocked down the fence, and walked through the break.

Old Mose became a legend in his own time. August Hall was gathering raspberries near Stirrup Ranch, and after filling his pails, he started back home. In the thickest portion of the bushes, he heard a snort. Not 50 yards away was Old Mose standing on his hind legs.

As stated by Hall:

> Suddenly my feet started running. No forethought had propelled them. Never before had I dreamed I was a born sprinter. As if by arrangement, my feet brought me to a

leaning spruce. Without slackening my speed until I reached the top, I 'pine-squirreled' up that spruce tree before the thought occurred to look back at the race — which should go down in the history of speed classics. After reaching the pinnacle of my objective, I looked down to find my 'inspiration' at the foot of my tree. He waddled around, attempting to start up the route I had opened through the thick limbs. Then, as if culling me out as dry meat after his feast on berries, he moseyed away leisurely.

Arriving home, my wife asked, 'What in the world have you done with your clothes?' Then for the first time I found I had little left of the clothing I wore at the time my feet spoke to me. 'I have just run Old Mose four miles,' I told her, not mentioning me being in the lead. My wife had to sit down to do her laughing. I tried to join her, but somehow the laugh wouldn't come.

Pigg knew the bear's range and estimated it took Old Mose around 30 days to make a round trip. Hunting is often cruel, and Pigg purchased a large steel trap. It was set by a shallow pond in a meadow where he always saw numerous tracks. Old Mose apparently splashed around in the water. Every morning, the trap was watched from a small hill overlooking the pond.

Just when Pigg figured the bear would return, the boy sent to check the trap returned to report that Old Mose was in the trap. The men at a nearby ranch ran for their guns and climbed the hill. The bear was gone, but his fresh tracks showed he had lost two toes from his left hind foot. The toes were found in the trap and were given to Beulah Beeler Evans who lived on the Beeler Ranch at the base of Black Mountain.

Old Mose was seen many times by a number of people and could now be easily identified by his tracks. He was big enough to kill cattle of any size and is credited with killing three full-grown bulls at one ranch. Some ranchers claimed that in the fall, just prior to hibernation, Old Mose weighed around 1,500 pounds.

In 1903, a professional hunter named James Anthony moved to Cañon City from Boise, Idaho. Anthony killed 16 bears during the previous year and more than 40 bears during his lifetime. He was introduced to Wharton Pigg, and the two men agreed to hunt Old Mose together. Anthony was a slim man with a thin mustache and cold, pale blue eyes. He also had a pack of well-trained dogs.

On their first day out in April 1904, Anthony and Pigg found the tracks of Old Mose and followed the trail for three days. The dogs finally struck a fresh scent. Old Mose had dined on a dead cow and then had gone into a thicket to rest between meals.

Pigg and Anthony split up; each took some of the dogs. The dogs that went with Pigg began to bark, but Pigg was partially deaf and may not have been able to hear them. Anthony, however, knew his dogs were on the bear's trail and ran to their location.

As put by Anthony:

> I soon came upon the dogs in a grove of quaking asp [sic] where they surrounded the biggest bear I ever saw in my life. At first he took no notice of me and paid but little attention to the dogs while he walked along, though they were pulling fur every minute. I fired at about seventy yards. Then I let go three more in succession, all of which were hits, but none fatal. He stood on his haunches and looked at me, dropped down and started for me.
>
> At about three yards, I took careful aim with my .30-40 Winchester. At this distance, bears generally make a rush upon a man.
>
> I got him between the eyes and he fell without a quiver. It took seven men to get him to the Stirrup Ranch, and we figured he weighed close to 1,000 pounds.

Anthony headed back to Cañon City with his dogs and wagon. Once he was gone, Wharton Pigg rode back to the site where "his bear" was killed and blazed the triangle of trees around the blood-stained ground. He carved on one tree, "Where Old Mose died," and on another, "Where J. W. Anthony stood when he fired the fatal shot." Up on the hillside on a thick aspen tree, Pigg carved "Old Mose's Last Bed" along with Anthony's name, his name, the names of the dogs in the pack and the date. Interesting enough, Pigg never returned to this spot nor did he reveal to his family that he was not the one who had killed the big grizzly.

A few days after Old Mose was killed, James Anthony boxed up the hide and skull and sent them to a taxidermy shop in Colorado Springs. He wanted them made into a rug with the mouth open. The hide was sent by the taxidermist to the Arvada Tannery where measurements were made by the editor of *Outdoor Life*. The bear measured 10 feet from the tip of the nose to its tail and nine-and-a-half feet from the front of one claw to the claw on the opposite side.

When Anthony left Cañon City and moved to Indiana, Old Mose went with him and hung on the wall of his home. Joseph Grinnell, at the University of California in Berkeley, wrote Anthony in 1920 asking that he donate the bear to the school. Grinnell told Anthony that the hide would be well protected and would be available for many years when knowledge of such animals as the grizzly could only be obtained from history.

After Anthony's death, Old Mose was sent to Berkeley. According to James Perkins in his excellent book, *Old Mose*, "If you are ever in Berkeley, California, why not drop in and see the old bear. He's catalogued as MVZ#113385. Tell him Jim Perkins sent you."

It was no surprise that after Old Mose was killed, Wharton Pigg fell into a state of depression. He didn't hold a grudge against James Anthony, and the two men remained friends. After Anthony left the Cañon City area in 1907, Pigg tried to build up a good pack of "bear" dogs. He also purchased a new and more powerful rifle. Try as he may, however, he never saw another grizzly bear.

Pigg eventually lost the Stirrup Ranch and was forced to homestead near Cover Mountain. Here he tried fox ranching, but this too failed. Eventually, he took a job with the U.S. Biological Service trapping coyotes. While trapping during the winter of 1930 near Walden, he was caught in a sudden snowstorm and nearly froze to death. He got an ear infection and was sent to Denver. The infection spread, and Wharton Pigg died on March 15, some 26 years after Old Mose was shot to death near Black Mountain.

James Perkins did extensive research into Old Mose and had one of the bear's teeth dated professionally. The bear that

KEN JESSEN

**No longer will the meadows around Black Mountain feel the weight of bears like Old Mose.** (Drawing by Kenneth Jessen)

was killed was in his prime and only 10 to 12 years old. Wharton Pigg had not been hunting the same bear for 20 years, and this bear could not have killed Jacob Radliff. The animal that was killed, however, was the last Black Mountain grizzly.

Grizzly bears have been hunted into extinction within Colorado, although some believe there are still a few left in the more remote areas of the San Juan Mountains. Bears such as Old Mose simply lived their lives as other bears had done for tens of thousands of years. Only mankind's desire to hunt them changed this picture. No longer will the meadows around Black Mountain feel the weight of a grizzly bear.

### References

Bair, Everett. *This Will Be an Empire*. New York: Pageant Press, 1959, pp. 252 260.

"Career of 'Old Mose,' a noted bear, is cut short." *Denver Republican*, May 3, 1904, p. 1.

Everett, George G., and Dr. Wendell F. Hutchinson. *Under the Angel of Shavano*. Denver: Golden Bell Press, 1963, pp. 257 261.

Perkins, James E. *Old Mose*. Manitou Springs, Colorado: Herodotus Press, 1991.

Queal, Cal. "The grizzly that terrorized Colorado." *Denver Post, Empire Magazine*, January 28, 1968, p. 3.

Sterling, Janet. "A true bear story." *Denver Post, Empire Magazine*, July 7, 1946.

Williams, Dr. Lester L. "Old Mose, the Great Grizzly." *Denver Westerners Golden Anniversary Brand Book*, Vol. XXXII. The Denver Posse of the Westerners, 1995, pp. 325 341.

Pat Lynch lived at the confluence of the Yampa and Green rivers. The area was named Echo Park by John Wesley Powell, but it was also known as Pat's Hole. (Colorado Historical Society)

# The Hermit of Pat's Hole

At the point where the Yampa River meets the Green River is a mile-long fin of rock, and the canyon walls are nearly vertical here. The Green River flows in opposite directions around this fin. John Wesley Powell named the area Echo Park because the opposing canyon walls created an extraordinary echo. As put by Powell, "Standing opposite the rock, our words are repeated with startling clearness, but in a soft, mellow tone that transforms them into magic music. Scarcely can you believe it is the echo of your own voice." This area also had another visitor, and another name.

Pat Lynch was born in Ireland and, as a teenage boy, worked on a sailing ship. He was shipwrecked on the coast of Africa and captured by a native tribe. After several years, he was rescued. He traveled to the United States, enlisted in the U.S. Navy under the name of James Cooper, and fought in the Civil War. He was badly wounded when trying to toss a live shell overboard after it landed on the deck of his ship. Later, he enlisted under his own name in the Union Army. After the Civil War ended, Pat Lynch drifted to Denver, then to Brown's Park. Lynch was hired to hunt game for Major Powell's survey party.

In 1883, Pat moved to the isolated northwestern corner of Colorado. Some say it was to escape prosecution for murder. For a short time, he lived in a cabin near the mouth of Hell's Canyon. While he was out getting some water, the cabin blew up. A possible cause could have been old dynamite stored in the cabin. Very suspicious by nature, Pat thought someone was after him, so he moved into a shelter cave along the Yampa River. He then started moving from cave to cave. During his occupation of each cave, he drew crude pictures of boats on the walls, much like Neolithic man.

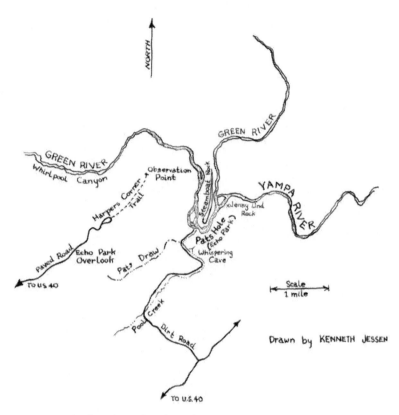

This shows the location of Pat's Hole.

(Map drawn by Kenneth Jessen)

Eventually, Lynch settled at the confluence of the Yampa and Green rivers between Lodore and Whirlpool canyons. The area named Echo Park by Powell became known as Pat's Hole. He constructed a lean-to covered with willow branches. This was all the shelter he had for many years until some local cowboys built a proper cabin for him.

Lynch didn't believe in killing animals, even though he had hunted at one time. He made pets of many of the wild creatures in the area, and he lived like a coyote by eating the flesh of dead animals he found in the river. He made jerky out of most of the meat. To allow him to travel light, he had jerky and bread cached throughout the area. When riding with a friend, he was known to stop and study the canyon for a minute. He would then walk over to a crack in the wall, or a rock, and recover some meat and bread. Naturally, some of it was pretty old.

Tales of Pat's close friendship with a mountain lion were widespread. He claimed he tamed this lion, and the big cat would frequently leave a dead deer by his cabin. He could call the lion with a peculiar wail. The lion would answer with a scream from the cliffs above Pat's Hole. Pat described the lion's scream by saying, "That sound is sweeter than any Jenny Lind ever sang." One of the cliffs in the area is now known as Jenny Lind Rock.

Lynch continued to maintain his little 25-acre ranch and planted a few peach trees. He also had a small garden and a couple of shacks. The bearded old man rode many miles to the nearest post office to collect his pension for service in the Civil War. He was fond of recounting his experiences to any visitor who would listen. Nearly deaf, he paid little attention to comments made by others during the middle of a good story. He kept up on the news by reading *New York World, Collier's Weekly* and the *Literary Digest*.

As he grew older, he scarcely knew what he was talking about. He rambled from one subject to the next. Visitors would listen with impatience to hear the end of some wonderful tale. Then he would suddenly switch to an entirely different subject, leaving the first story unfinished.

Pat was constantly drawing sailing vessels. Some of his drawings are carved into the canyon walls. His body was elaborately tattooed. When he was in the right mood, he told people he killed a man in Pittsburgh and fled to the West to escape punishment. It may have been a joke or a means of shocking visitors.

During the last three years of his life, the hermit of Pat's Hole lived with friends. He died in 1917 at the age of 98.

After Pat's death, a small scrap of paper was found in one of the caves he occupied on Upper Pool Creek. Written on the paper was the following message:

To all who this may consarn [sic] that I Pat Lynch do
lay claim on this bottom for my home and support this 8th
month of 1886

(signed) P. Lynch

If in these caverns you shelter take
Plais [sic] do to them no harm
Love everything you find around
Hanging up or on the ground.

**References**

McMechen, Edgar C. "The Hermit of Pat's Hole." *Colorado Magazine*, XIX,
No. 3 (May 1942), pp. 91 98.

# The Legends of the Great Sand Dunes

The scientific explanation of why the Great Sand Dunes are
located at the base of the Sangre de Cristo Mountains is
quite simple. The arid floor of the San Luis Valley is sparsely
covered with vegetation. The prevailing winds blow from the
west across the valley picking up loose grains of sand. The
grains bounce across the valley floor toward the Sangre de
Cristos. The mountains form a 6,000-foot barrier with the
exception of the area north of Blanca Peak where Music,
Medano and Mosca passes are located. The wind is funneled
toward this low area, and as it rises over the mountains, it loses
much of its energy. The wind can no longer carry all of the
sand, and it is dropped. Over thousands of years, the Great
Sand Dunes were slowly formed.

The dunes are quite strange. They rise abruptly more than 700
feet above their surroundings and extend for 10 miles along the
base of the mountains. The wind causes the sand to constantly

shift against the fixed backdrop of the rugged Sangre de Cristos. In the process, the lower part of the forest is being slowly buried. Flowing along the edge of the dunes is Medano Creek. Water spreads out over the bed of sand in pulsations called bores.

Long before a scientific explanation for the dunes existed, however, mankind was compelled to offer some reason for their presence. This led to a variety of legends. The earliest account of how these great dunes were formed may be the following story, which appeared in the August 6, 1885, issue of the *Alamosa Journal*.

A party of men camped near the great dunes in 1885. During dinner, a Spaniard entered the camp. As he drew near the light from the fire, the men could see that he had long, black, curly hair that fell from beneath a broad-brimmed sombrero. He had large black eyes, a narrow chin, and his mouth was partially hidden by a black moustache. He stood over six feet tall, and the men guessed that he was around 40 years old. In his hand was a Winchester rifle, and a Colt .45 revolver was stuck in his cartridge belt. As he stepped toward the fire, he greeted the men with, "Buenos tardes, señores."

The men welcomed him in Spanish and invited him to stay. He was asked if he understood English, and he said he did. He introduced himself as Francis Gonzalez. He added that he was from New Mexico, where he owned a large hacienda. The reason he came to the San Luis Valley was to hunt elk, but now he found himself 20 miles from his camp. The men asked him to spend the night.

One of the men expressed curiosity about how the great dunes of sand were formed. For a moment Gonzalez remained silent, then, gazing into the campfire, said,

Señor, if it would please you, I can relate to you how the famous sand dunes of the San Luis Valley really came into existence. There are undoubtedly many who can tell you this tale, but there is no one living who would be more apt to know the truth in regard to it than myself for it was my grandfather who started the formation of the largest one in the range with part of his herd of sheep and several of his herders.

The eyes of the men lit up with wild enthusiasm, and they begged Gonzalez to continue with his story.

The Spaniard began:

It's been 10 years if not more since I last repeated what I am to tell you tonight, and although it may seem almost incredible to you, it is, nevertheless, true. What I am to repeat to you was told to me by my father and has been told by me to my children.

It was the year 1816 that my grandfather, Don Louis Gonzalez, returned to his home in Mexico where he had enormous herds of cattle and sheep. He had developed his herd by making trips north into New Mexico and southern Colorado.

He had penetrated into this part of Colorado and had traveled over the San Luis Valley. Feed was here in such abundance that my grandfather returned to his home completely charmed with this part of the world and was fully determined to brave Indians and hardships...to send a small portion of his herd of sheep, in (the) charge of some of his Mexican herders, to this valley. He, therefore, selected 3,500 sheep from his herd, picked out five of his most trusty herders, and sent them upon their journey. They traveled many hundred leagues, and it was in the springtime that they arrived at their destination.

They immediately set to work building cabins to live in and corrals for the sheep. A month had passed away and the sheep were thriving wonderfully, and nothing had occurred to give them warning of their approaching doom.

On the twenty-fifth of June, one herder, Martinez by name, proposed to go over the mountains and see what kind of country lay on the other side. He started out during the fairest of weather and passed through Mosca Pass. After three days spent in wandering around the eastern side of the range he started to return to his companions. He pursued his way through the pass with no foreboding of the horrible fate that had overtaken those left behind, and at last arrived at the mouth of the pass.

He looked, and where he should have seen the newly erected cabins and the herd peacefully grazing, he saw only an immense mountain of sand. He was dumbfounded and could not believe it at first...or else he had lost his way and his companions, with the sheep, were off in some other direction. After going a short distance farther and seeing many familiar landmarks, he at last came to realize what had happened: Where now stood only a large hill of sand was where his home had been for the last month.

He started immediately to find his brother herders, but after searching for them for two days he gave them up as lost. A storm had risen during his absence and buried the 3,500 sheep, his four companions, their houses, and corrals beneath fifty feet of sand. That was the beginning of the famous sand dunes of Colorado. The herder who had escaped the fate of his companions then set out to carry the news to my grandfather, and after encountering many hardships, he at last arrived at the hacienda and related to his master all he knew.

Sandstorms year after year have kept piling the sand in this heap until, today, it stands fully 800 feet high above the bones of those who perished there...years ago.

Hill after hill was formed from that, until now there exists a chain extending many miles up the valley. A search was made for the bodies of the Mexicans who perished there, but before laborers could succeed in getting ten feet below the surface, the excavation made would completely fill with the loose sand, and the undertaking was abandoned.

The Great Sand Dunes National Park includes dunes that rise over 700 feet above the floor of the San Luis Valley. The sand is ever drifting, driven by prevailing winds from the west. (Kenneth Jessen)

After Señor Gonzalez finished his tale of how the great sand dunes were started, he rolled himself up in his blanket and fell fast asleep leaving his companions to ponder the truth about the mysterious, evershifting sand dunes.

Another story on the romantic side appears in Luther Bean's *Land of the Blue Sky People*. A Spanish-speaking family settled at the mouth of a small creek near Fort Massachusetts,

Medano Creek flows over a bed of sand at the base of the dunes. The water washes over the sand in pulsations called bores. This is just one of the strange features of the dunes. (Kenneth Jessen)

located at the base of the Sangre de Cristo Mountains. The father and his son, Benito, farmed the arid land and raised sheep. The sheep belonged to the farmer's rich older brother.

A Ute chief came to their home one day with a young girl. The chief wanted to sell her and said that she was stolen from the Navajos to the south. She did not have any Indian features, however. The farmer reasoned that the girl was part of a white family on the Huerfano River that had been killed in an ambush. The farmer believed that the girl was spared and taken captive, a common practice among the Ute Indians. The farmer borrowed money from his brother and purchased the girl. She was too young to talk and could not verify the chief's story. The farmer and his wife named her Paulita, and as she grew up, she began helping Benito with herding the rich brother's sheep.

As she became a teenager, she grew to be a beautiful woman. The Ute chief, now much older, would come back periodically to see the girl. It was obvious to the farmer that he wanted her back for his own. But the rich brother, also lusted for the girl. The farmer knew that if he gave the girl to his brother, his debts would be forgiven.

In order to get Benito out of the way, the brother ordered him to take the flock to grass growing north of the ranch near the Great Sand Dunes. Paulita knew that Benito was on a dangerous mission, for sandstorms ravaged the area. Men and their entire flocks had been buried alive by the choking sand. Paulita would leave the farmer and climb a hill to look toward the dunes, worried about Benito.

One day when she was away, the chief returned. He was in a bad mood and demanded the young girl. He camped near the farmer's home, and when Paulita returned later in the day, the farmer warned her of the chief's intentions. She immediately took the old chief's horse and a bearskin coat, and rode north toward the dunes after Benito. When the chief woke up the next morning, he discovered his horse gone. He took an old pack horse and took out after the girl. The rich brother came by a few minutes later, also wanting the young girl. When the farmer told him about the chief, he took a young, wild bronco from the corral. His mount was exhausted. The bronco threw the brother several times before he gained control over the animal.

Now the chase was on. The rich brother was gaining on the old chief. Paulita was far in the lead. As a storm came up, the rich brother rode up to the chief. The chief used his bow and arrow to shoot at the brother. The arrow struck home, but as the brother fell from his saddle, he got off a shot with his revolver. The Indian also was fatally wounded, and the two men fell to the ground and died. The blowing sand soon covered the bodies.

In the meantime, Benito was crossing over the dunes to a stand of cottonwoods. He reached the trees before the storm overtook him. He lay down with his pack animals and protected their noses from the blowing sand. He huddled under a blanket. The fury of the storm let up momentarily, and he heard a horse's whinny. Soon he saw Paulita riding through the blowing sand. She crawled in under the blanket with him, and they waited out the storm. When the air cleared, the pack animals were alive as well as part of the herd of sheep. The couple rode over the mountains and settled near the headwaters of the Huerfano River. They lived happily ever after and never talked about the incident that happened to them. Years later, the bones of the brother and the chief were uncovered by drifting sand.

**References**

Bean, Luther E. *Land of the Blue Sky People*. Self published, 1975, pp. 95 97.
"The disappearing sheep of the Sand Dunes." *Alamosa Journal*, August 6, 1885. (republished in *The San Luis Valley Historian*, Vol. XIV, No. 2 (Spring, 1982), pp. 2528.)
Trimble, Stephen A. *Great Sand Dunes*. Globe, Arizona: Southwest Parks and Monuments Association, 1978.

Jefferson Randolph 'Soapy' Smith was probably Colorado's greatest con artist. He and his mob operated in Denver, Leadville and Creede. He got the name Soapy from a confidence game involving small bars of soap.

(Denver Public Library, Western History Department)

# Soapy Smith

In the late nineteenth century, Jefferson Randolph Smith, better known as "Soapy" Smith, and his gang of confidence men operated freely near Denver's Union Station. Beginning in 1885, Soapy Smith had a gentleman's agreement with Denver authorities not to rob or molest its citizens. In exchange, he and his men were allowed to con the unsuspecting out-of-towners out of every cent they had.

Soapy Smith organized the "bandit barbers" of Seventeenth Street. They lured strangers into their shop by advertising a shave and haircut for only 25 cents. While the unsuspecting customer's eyes were covered with a steaming hot towel, the barber would flip the sign over to read $1. The customer was in no position to protest with a razor at his throat. This wasn't the end of the fleecing, however. If the victim had a fat wallet, the barber would deftly snip an inverted "V" at the hairline on the back of the neck. As the marked man left the barbershop, another member of Soapy's gang would spot the mark and try to take him for an even more costly trimming.

Soapy Smith was one of Colorado's unforgettable characters. He had brown hair, a Vandyke beard and a silvery voice. His most famous con was to stand in front of his small folding table at a corner along Larimer Street and attract a crowd with his repertoire of stories mixed with quick-witted comments. As he talked, he would twist a $10, $20 or even a $100 bill around a common bar of soap. He then wrapped the soap in a blue piece of paper. The crowd watched intently as he tossed the bar into a pile of identically wrapped bars on his small table. Next, he would invite the crowd to step right up and take a chance on winning "one of these little green papers with big numbers" for the ridiculous price of $5. A shill would be the first to step for-

Soapy Smith is seen standing in the center of the bar in his Skagway, Alaska, saloon. (Denver Public Library, Western History Department)

ward and pay the $5. Naturally, he would get one of the bars wrapped with a bill. Anxious buyers would press forward handing $5 bills to Soapy as fast as he could take the money. Few ended up with anything more than a nickel cake of common toilet soap. In a way, it was an "honest" con, and Soapy would caution the crowd to watch him carefully. His famous expression was, "Use the soap to wash away your sins! Cleanliness is next to Godliness, but the feel of a crisp greenback in the pocket is paradise."

Soapy had an office on the second floor of a three-story brick building at Seventeenth and Larimer streets. Some of his cons required elaborate props, an office and some great acting. He could pass himself off as a big investor in an atmosphere of dignified elegance, or some other role as required by the situation.

Soapy Smith took advantage of the greed of others, and in situations where honest people needed his help, he was more than happy to offer a hand. At Christmas, Soapy would stand at Seventeenth and Market streets and hand out turkeys to Denver's poor.

At one o'clock in the morning just a few days before Christmas, Parson Tom Uzzell heard knocking at his door. The parson opened the door and standing there was none other than Jefferson Randolph Smith. In a moment, the great con man had dumped $5,500 in gold and greenbacks on the hall floor at the parson's feet. Soapy had won it at his favorite game, faro. After reading about how the parson needed funds for Christmas, Soapy decided to give up his winnings. The money was used to feed the poor at the People's Tabernacle on Christmas day. Later, Parson Uzzell invited Soapy to deliver a sermon. It was titled, "Look Not Upon Evil," and was well received.

As Denver matured, its citizens became fed up with Soapy's mob rule. The handwriting was on the wall, and Soapy left for the new silver camp of Creede in 1892. The rough and tumble town was ripe for a takeover. It was easy for Soapy to make friends in a town that was gaining people at the rate of 300 per day. Many had heard of him from Denver, and he was welcomed as a celebrity. Always well dressed in his black suit and hat, Soapy became the underworld leader of Creede.

Soapy was able to maintain law and order in Creede without interfering with his own business. The headquarters for his gang was the Orleans Club. Those who came to Creede on legitimate business were welcomed by Smith, but those who tried to horn in on his rackets were dispensed with quickly. A great deal of money flowed into Soapy's pockets, and had he possessed any propensity to save, he would have ended up a rich man.

One day, a poor preacher came into the camp and began preaching from a street corner. This man of the cloth found the going rough because of the noise and disrespectful comments made by the crowd of miners. Soapy took pity on him and marched through the crowd. "Speak up, parson," Soapy said, "Creede needs a little religion. We'll back you to the limit. The town is yours." Soapy turned to some of his men and added,

"Boys, we are all going to church next Sunday, and in the meantime, we are going to raise money so this man can have a church house here." Soapy's mob began visiting saloons, parlor houses, gambling halls and other places in town. After about two hours, they delivered $600 into the hands of the dumbfounded parson. A small, clapboard church was erected quickly, and Soapy Smith, with a few of his men, attended the first service.

Creede was the type of boomtown that had an around-the-clock carnival atmosphere. It was the perfect setting for an inventive hoax. An imaginative fellow, Bob Fitzsimmons, found a cement body of a man in a Denver warehouse. Possibly it was the old Solid Muldoon (a hoax perpetrated in 1877 and backed by P. T. Barnum). Fitzsimmons had it shipped to Creede in a box, and during the night, he hauled it a short distance from town. He buried it in the mud along Farmer's Creek. The cement man "aged" for a few days until it was "discovered" by a friend of Fitzsimmons. The discovery was reported in the local paper of April 15, 1892. Heralded as the most perfect and interesting "petrification" ever found, the cement body was hauled back to Creede and put on display at the Vaughn Hotel. Hundreds of curious people paid a quarter to view it.

Jefferson Randolph "Soapy" Smith was fascinated by what he quickly recognized as a good hoax. He watched for a while, but the sound of all that silver changing hands was just too much for him to resist. By manipulation, he became the owner of "Colonel Stone." This transfer of property was certainly not straightforward and was reported in the *Creede Candle* as follows:

> Jeff Smith has purchased the petrified man and will travel with him. The price was $3,000. Jeff paid the money this morning and went down to get possession. Four others claimed ownership, and it required some lively discussion with fists and guns to get away with it.

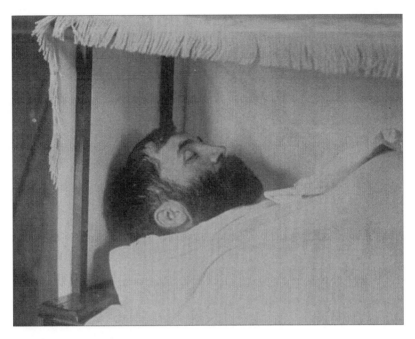

Soapy Smith and Frank Reid shot it out in July 1898, on Skagway, Alaska's, main street. Both men perished in the gunfight. Soapy looks peaceful in this Skagway mortuary. (Denver Public Library, Western History Department)

Soapy was much more of a showman than the former owner of the petrified man. He moved the cement figure into his Orleans Club and placed it in a dark area. The figure was illuminated using kerosene lamps. To create an eerie effect, the flues were partially blackened, and the lamps were exposed to a slight draft to cause the flame to flicker and cast strange shadows on the figure. The dim light also was necessary because the figure was beginning to crumble.

Naturally, Soapy gave lectures about the figure to increase attendance at the attraction. The cement man had now become a prehistoric monster. Soapy talked about the creation of man and how over the centuries, he had evolved into a new kind of body. This justified the cement man's different shape.

After Soapy had milked the petrified man for every silver coin it would yield, he leased it to a circus, and the figure toured the United States. When it returned, Soapy sold it to a fellow promoter.

Eventually, the Smith regime in Creede ended, and Soapy moved to Skagway, Alaska. He tried to take over this town and was shot to death in 1898 by a member of an opposing gang. He was only 38 years old and left behind just $250.

**References**

Blair, Edward. *Everybody Came to Leadville*. Leadville, Colorado: Timberline Books, 1971, pp. 29 30.

Collier, William Ross, and Edwin Victor Westrate. *The Reign of Soapy Smith*. New York: Doubleday, 1935.

Feitz, Leland. *Soapy Smith's Creede*. Colorado Springs, Colorado: Little London Press, 1973.

Hunt, Inez, and Wanetta W. Draper. *To Colorado's Restless Ghosts*. Denver: Sage Books, 1960, pp. 34 40.

Robertson, Frank G., and Beth Kay Harris. *Soapy Smith: King of the Frontier Con Men*. New York: Hastings House, 1961.

Smith, Joseph Emerson. "Personal Recollections of Early Denver." *Colorado Magazine*, XX, No. 2 (March 1943), pp. 60 61.

# Trackless Train

During the winter months, the vast floor of South Park becomes frozen tundra. High winds, blowing snow and sub-zero temperatures combine to obliterate the features of this high valley. Surrounded by peaks over 14,000 feet, South Park spawns some of the most severe weather conditions in the Rocky Mountains. In the summer, however, the high meadows form a lush carpet for grazing cattle and antelope.

Livestock must be kept moving during the winter, and they must be fed regularly to survive. During the days when the Denver, South Park & Pacific operated its diminutive narrow-gauge trains through the park, the cattle had favorite crossings. The many footfalls of cattle would pack snow between the rails.

A Denver, South Park & Pacific train quietly left the tracks during a ground blizzard and traveled across the frozen expanse of South Park for some distance before stopping in front of a haystack. (Rendering by Kenneth Jessen)

Eventually, the snow would be compressed into solid ice between the rails and could easily derail a train.

In February 1885, a long train of empty cars pulled by a small locomotive left Como for the Baldwin coal mines north of Gunnison. The weather was extremely cold, and the wind whipped the snow across the bleak, rolling floor of South Park. The blowing snow hugged the ground and obscured every detail. Unexpectedly, the engineer saw an ominous shape in the distance. As the train got closer, it turned out to be a large haystack. The engineer quickly applied the brakes and brought the train to a stop. The ranchers were always doing dumb things like putting haystacks wherever it suited them, thought the engineer.

The train crew walked from the caboose and joined the engineer to view the obstacle, and if possible, remove it from the right-of-way. They examined the haystack, and then glanced down at the ground. Something was missing: the rails! There weren't any rails under the locomotive or, for that matter, under any portion of the train! In fact, no rails were seen anywhere, even in the distance. The train had quietly left the twin bands of steel at an ice-packed cattle crossing and was traveling across the frozen ground. The haystack saved the engineer from continuing across South Park.

A crew member was sent back to the nearest station to get help. It was some time before the train could be towed back to the track because of the length of cable required.

The Denver, South Park & Pacific was absorbed into the Union Pacific system and was renamed the Denver, Leadville & Gunnison. The U.P. went bankrupt and the narrow-gauge line was taken over by the Colorado & Southern in 1898. In 1938, most of the old Denver, South Park & Pacific was scrapped.

References

Poor, M. C. *Denver, South Park & Pacific*. Denver: Rocky Mountain Railroad Club, 1976, p. 368.

# Miner's Companion Is His Violin

High above the mining town of Silver Plume, a rich vein of ore was discovered in the late 1860s by Clifford Griffin. This young Englishman was one of the first miners to come to the Silver Plume area. Little was known about him except that his fiancée had been found dead on the eve of their wedding. Griffin came to the Rocky Mountains to enter the mining business and to forget his sad past.

Griffin discovered a rich vein of ore and named his mine the Seven-thirty. It contained both silver and gold. The deeper the mine was developed, the richer the ore. The young Englishman soon became the wealthiest mine owner in the area. Nothing, however, caused him to forget his fiancée's untimely death, and he withdrew socially from the other miners and their families.

On the side of the steep mountain near his mine, Griffin constructed a simple cabin. His sole companion was his violin, and after the end of a day's work, he would stand at the front of his cabin and play. The sad music would drift down into Silver Plume, and miners and their families would come outside and look up to see the lonely musician by his cabin. Sometimes one of the miners would request a special tune. After he completed his mountainside recital, the miners would applaud with the sound echoing off the canyon walls.

Directly in front of his cabin, Griffin dug a grave in the solid rock. One spring evening in 1887, he played especially well. The miners applauded, then watched him walk toward the grave. Suddenly, the sharp report of a gun reverberated through the hills. Clifford Griffin was found face down in his own grave with a bullet through the heart.

In his cabin was a note requesting that he be left in the stone

High above Silver Plume this impressive granite shaft marks the grave of Clifford Griffin. After playing a sad song on his violin, Griffin shot himself and fell into his own grave. (Kenneth Jessen)

grave. The miners not only followed his last instructions but erected a granite marker over the grave with the following inscription:

Clifford Griffin Son of Alfred Griffin Esq. of Brand Hull, Shropshire, England Born July 2, 1847 Died June 19, 1887 and in Consideration of His Own Request Buried Here

**References**

Bueler, Gladys R. *Colorado's Colorful Characters*. Boulder, Colorado: Pruett Publishing Co., 1981, p 33.

Wolle, Muriel Sibell. *Stampede to Timberline*. Chicago: The Swallow Press, 1949, p. 128.

Lyulph "Lord" Ogilvy as he looked during his youth. He is in the center with two unidentified companions.

(Denver Public Library, Western History Department)

# Lord Ogilvy

Captain The Honorable Lyulph Gilchrist Stanley Ogilvy, D.S.O., was born in London, in 1861, to the Eighth Earl of Airlie. His father brought him to Colorado in 1889, at which time the Earl of Airlie purchased the 3,500-acre SLW Ranch in the northeastern part of the state. The ranch was turned over to the 28-year-old Lyulph to manage.

Ogilvy discovered freedom in the American West, far different from the formalities imposed on him at home. He was well educated, but at the same time, possessed a certain earthy quality usually not associated with an aristocratic background. Ogilvy stood straight and tall at six-foot-two, but had a sense of mischief. In the words of author Bill Hosokawa, "Legends clustered around Ogilvy the way barnacles attach themselves to a ship's hull."

The ranch was located in an isolated part of Colorado, and Ogilvy needed occasional company. For this reason, he frequented the Windsor Hotel in Denver. Here he developed a group of comrades inclined toward the wholesale consumption of liquid refreshments. One story tells of a meeting with Buffalo Bill Cody at the Windsor. Ogilvy remained at the bar beyond the time of departure of the last train north. To solve his need for transportation, he spotted a steamroller near the hotel and drove it to his ranch near Fort Morgan, a distance of more than 80 miles. As the story goes, the trip took most of the night, and Ogilvy would stop the slow-moving piece of machinery for fuel and water along the way. Most of the bridges were wooden, and due to the ponderous weight of Ogilvy's newly acquired vehicle, they later had to be condemned.

Years after this story appeared, his son, Jack, set the record straight by saying that it was not a steamroller, but rather a steam tractor of equal size. It was purchased by Ogilvy to dig a ditch near Fort Morgan. Jack says his father drove the noisy machine home at night to keep from spooking teams. The bridges had to be replaced, but in Lyulph's mind, they needed rebuilding anyway.

The Windsor Hotel remembered Ogilvy for years to come. When they failed to awaken him one morning, he returned with a number of cockerels that were just learning to crow. He released them at five in the morning and woke many of the guests. He also drove two ponies, hitched together, into the hotel lobby.

Many of Ogilvy's escapades involved horses. He owned and raced horses, rode in the steeplechase and participated in fox hunts. His prize horse was Trooper, who *Post*ed a win at Denver's Overland Park during the late 1880s. After the win, Ogilvy invited his friends to his ranch to honor Trooper. He meant this literally; when his guests arrived, there was Trooper standing at the head of the receiving line! To demonstrate the ability of this fine animal, Ogilvy stacked chairs and couches in the center of the room and had Trooper hurdle them. Trooper, however, was not accustomed to being indoors and refused to leave the house. Ogilvy had to remove a section of one wall to return Trooper to his stall.

When Lady Maud, Ogilvy's sister, came to visit, she was met at the depot. Ogilvy used a couple of unbroken two-year-old horses to pull the surrey. When Lady Maud climbed aboard, the horses bolted into a dead run. During the whirlwind trip to Ogilvy's ranch, Lady Maud didn't say a word. Near the ranch, the vehicle careened madly, and one of the wheels splintered. The surrey almost turned over and came to rest against a tree. Lady Maud stepped serenely down and remarked to her brother, "What a charming place you have, Lyulph."

Later during her visit, she was traveling by stagecoach in California. She was invited to sit next to the driver on the box. On a steep hill with tight switchbacks, brakes smoking, the driver turned to Lady Maud and said, "Ain't you just a little bit afraid?" Calling upon her past experiences, she replied, "I'm used to driving with my brother."

During his early years, Lyulph Ogilvy was reflecting with one of his friends on the brevity of life. They were standing along Larimer Street in Denver as a funeral procession went by. Still recovering from the effects of an excessive amount of liquor the night before, they bet on which one of them would be the principal in such an event. To win the bet, Ogilvy paid an undertaker $1,000 to arrange for the most spectacular funeral Denver had ever seen. A brass band, mourners and a parade were part of the deal. Besides, the interior of the padded coffin looked quite comfortable, and Ogilvy felt a strong need to lie down.

At 20th and Larimer streets and in mid-afternoon, the parade was assembled. Everything went well until the wagon hit a rut at 16th Street and jarred the coffin. The "corpse" howled at the driver, "Take it easy!"

The driver apparently was not let in on the prank and let out a yell as he jumped from the wagon. The horses took off at a dead run, and the coffin fell out on the street. Ogilvy pulled himself out of the splintered wreckage. At the Windsor Hotel that evening, there was a party of even greater magnitude than the one the night before.

During his days of running the ranch, Ogilvy had a house-keeper by the name of Mrs. Wilson. To keep her company, she had a cat, but this animal epitomized feline meanness. Ogilvy owned a bull terrier named Cute. The cat would drive Cute away from his food even though the cat was well fed. When Cute was sleeping, the cat would climb on his back and work its claws into the dog's skin.

Ogilvy kindly suggested to Mrs. Wilson that sooner or later, Cute would lose control and take it out on the cat. Mrs. Wilson replied, "Oh no, Mr. Ogilvy, Cute loves that cat." But Mrs. Wilson failed to estimate Cute's tolerance level. Also, Cute knew better than to show any hostility in the presence of Mrs. Wilson. Patience paid off, and Cute caught the cat away from the safety of the house. He tore the cat from limb to limb shredding its body.

Lord Ogilvy during his later years working for the *Denver Post* as their
farm and livestock writer. (Denver Public Library, Western History Department)

Ogilvy discovered what was left of Mrs. Wilson's cat and gathered up the pieces in a scoop. He buried it far from the house and did not mention the matter to her. When the cat failed to show up, Mrs. Wilson was sure it had fallen prey to a coyote.

Eventually, Ogilvy got married and had two children. His wife became ill, and in order to pay her medical expenses, he was forced to sell his property. He ended up working in Denver for $1.50 a night as a watchman in the railroad yards. Harry Tammen, co-owner of the *Denver Post*, knew Ogilvy during his younger years. He spotted Ogilvy at the railroad yards and knew of his extensive knowledge of livestock, ranching and farming. Tammen hired Ogilvy on the spot as his farm and livestock writer. At the age of 48, Ogilvy was given his own desk at the *Post* and, in turn, gave the newspaper a certain air of respectability. Ogilvy held this job until the age of 83.

Tammen said to Ogilvy, "To hell with calling yourself 'Lyulph.' I wouldn't know what it meant in a thousand years. You're the son of an Earl, ain't you? Well, you're going to work for me, and you're going to be 'Lord Ogilvy' to me whether you like it or not." And so Lyulph was known as Lord Ogilvy from then on.

Lord Ogilvy used to explain to his co-workers that he was a Scot and that his clansmen fought among themselves mostly for exercise and for the sheer joy of living. Whenever the English would invade Scotland from the south, the clan would stop fighting one another and lick the English. Afterwards, the Ogilvy clan would resume their own internal warfare.

It was the custom of the clan to travel lightly in the field. They took rations of only oatmeal and slept wherever the day's battle ended. One of his relatives had a son of about 18. At the time, they were engaged in a major battle with the English. At the close of the day, the senior Ogilvy was making the rounds in camp to see how his son had fared during his first conflict. He came upon the boy sound asleep on the ground with his head resting on a cold rock. Infuriated, the father kicked the rock from under the boy's head and remarked, "Let it never be said that a son of mine was reared in the lap of luxury!"

Lord Ogilvy died at the age of 85 in a Boulder nursing home. He served in the Spanish-American War, the Boer War (where he was awarded the Distinguished Service Order) and in World War I.

### References
Baskett, Floyd. "Mrs. Winston Churchill's legendary Uncle Lyulph." *Denver Post, Empire Magazine*, April 1957, pp. 12 13.

Fowler, Gene. *Timberline*. New York: Garden City Publishing Co., 1947, pp. 110 114.

Hosokawa, Bill. *Thunder in the Rockies*. New York: William Morrow & Co., 1976, pp. 85 93.

Ogilvy, J. D. A. "Certain Adventures of L. Ogilvy." *Denver Post, Empire Magazine*, October 18, 1970, pp. 8 11.

Ogilvy, J. D. A. "As a horseman he convinced the cowboys." *Denver Post, Empire Magazine*, October 25, 1970, pp. 41 45.

Parkhill, Forbes. *The Wildest of the West*. New York: Henry Holt and Co., 1951, pp. 124 126.

# The Hanging Flume

The story of one of the most spectacular engineering feats in the history of Colorado began during the 1880s when prospectors discovered a placer deposit of finely powdered gold on Mesa Creek Flats above the Dolores River four miles below its junction with the San Miguel River. The flow of water from Mesa Creek was so small, however, that panning operations were restricted to the spring and early summer. Nearly every pan contained some fine gold flakes, and it was believed that if more water could be brought into Mesa Creek Flats to support hydraulic mining, a fortune could be made.

This led to the construction of one of the most unique structures in Colorado history—a flume suspended on a vertical sandstone cliff high above the Dolores and San Miguel rivers.

Capitalists from St. Louis formed the Montrose Placer Mining Company. It was managed by Col. N. P. Turner, an experienced mining man who knew that the first task was to bring water into the area from the San Miguel. The river was a dozen miles away, and Turner proposed to carry the water by a combination of a ditch and flume.

Hydraulic mining uses large nozzles to wash the gold-bearing gravel into a sluice for recovery of gold dust. The water requirements for this type of mining are substantial. A sluice looks very much like a flume and is placed at an angle sufficient to allow gravel and sand to pass through. There are small boards called riffles nailed across the bottom of the flume at right angles to the water flow. They trap the heavier gold particles. At the beginning of each shift, the miner places a small amount of mercury in each riffle. Gold is absorbed or amalgamated into the mercury. The amalgamation from each riffle is recovered at the end of the shift, and the gold is separated from the mercury. The mercury then is placed back in the riffles.

The water diversion project was started in 1889, and completed two years later. The intake point was on the San Miguel River near the present-day town of Uravan. The project required a flume eight miles long on the northern wall of San Miguel Canyon, four feet deep and six feet wide to carry the necessary volume of water. The flume was supported by brackets embedded in the side of the vertical sandstone cliffs. The flume varied from 100 to 150 feet above the riverbed and 250 to 500 feet below the rim of the gorge. This spectacular structure ran a mile and a half on the cliffs above the San Miguel River and more than six miles on the canyon wall above the Dolores River.

The flume required a great deal of milled lumber. The Montrose Placer Mining Company set up a sawmill just across the state line in Utah to provide the lumber. Pine boards, two inches thick, were hauled by wagon to the construction site. In all, an estimated 1.8-million board-feet of lumber were used in this project.

To construct the flume, a flat car on a temporary track nailed into the flume was used. The flat car was equipped with a long crane at one end and a counter weight of rocks at the other end. Workmen were held over the canyon wall while they drilled holes in the sandstone for the iron brackets. After a bracket was in place, a section of flume was constructed. The tracks on the flume bed were advanced, the flat car was pushed ahead and the next bracket was installed. In some places, men were lowered over the side of the rim to drill the holes and install the brackets. The grade of the flume was held to a steady six feet 10 inches per mile.

Men were paid $2.50 a day, and about 25 were assigned to work on the flume.

To get the milled lumber to the flume, either it was hoisted from the canyon floor with ropes or lowered over the canyon rim. Some material was floated by barge down the river to the construction site.

The rotting remains of the hanging flume still cling to the sandstone cliffs.
The flume can be viewed from Colorado Highway 141 near Uravan.

(Kenneth Jessen)

The cost of the great flume was over $100,000, and the project was completed in the early summer of 1891. Water flowed the entire distance in fine shape and was delivered at the rate of 80-million gallons per day.

The stockholders in the Montrose Placer Mining Company, had high hopes of becoming rich. It was estimated that the gravel on Mesa Creek Flats would yield 25 cents to 35 cents per cubic yard of material. The capacity of the operation allowed the company to wash 4,000 to 5,000 cubic yards of gravel per day, and the yield should have amounted to well over a $1,000 a day.

The placer miners who discovered the gold on Mesa Creek Flats had little difficulty recovering it with their pans. When the gold-bearing sand was sent through a sluice, the gold was so fine that it washed right through and remained suspended in the water. It became clear that the entire investment in the flume was lost. Turner became so disheartened over the complete failure of the project that he went to Chicago, rented a room and shot himself through the head.

The flume soon was abandoned. Ranchers salvaged as much lumber as they could to build houses, sheds and barns. The rotting remains of the fabulous San Miguel flume still cling to the sandstone cliffs above the Dolores and San Miguel rivers. The flume can be viewed from Colorado Highway 141 near Uravan.

References
Rockwell, Wilson. *Uncompahgre Country*. Denver: Sage Books, 1965,
    pp. 160 166.

# Denver's City Hall War

Republicans wanted their fair share of the spoils in Denver's corrupt city government, and the Fire and Police Board was created in the city's seventh session. It became known as the "Robber Seventh." since the gambling elements made arrangements with the police. It was common knowledge that con artists had an "arrangement" with Denver police: if they plied their trade on new arrivals near Denver's Union Station, they would go unmolested. Possibly some protection money was paid to the police. Con artist and gambler Jefferson Randolph "Soapy" Smith was one of the primary crime bosses.

Along comes a former Aspen newspaper editor, Davis H. Waite. He was a reformer who wanted to clean up Denver. Elected in 1892 as Colorado's governor, he ordered that gambling and other illicit activities stop. When two members of the Fire and Police Board would not enforce the law, Governor Waite ordered their removal. The men in question were seasoned politicians Jackson Orr and D. J. Martin, who immediately refused to vacate their offices. Waite presented evidence that Orr and Martin provided police protection for an unnamed gambling den.

Earlier in his career as governor, Waite had proposed several ridiculous schemes, including having Colorado coin its own silver dollars. The price of silver had been falling, and in 1893, the Sherman Silver Purchase Act was repealed. The act had required the United States to purchase a fixed amount of silver every year. Its repeal sent silver prices even lower and resulted in a recession that closed the majority of Colorado silver mines. Since the U.S. government had a monopoly on coinage, Waite's plan was to ship Colorado silver to Mexico for minting. They were termed "fandango dollars." and the scheme never materialized.

Gov. Davis H. Waite, a reformer, wanted to clean up Denver by eliminating its gambling halls. When two members of the Fire and Police Board refused his orders, he demanded they step down. (Library of Congress)

Waite called out the Colorado militia and sent 300 soldiers down Lawrence Street on March 14, 1894, to physically remove two members of the Denver City Fire and Police Board. (Denver Public Library, Western History Department)

In March 1894, Waite expanded his demands to include the removal of two members of the Denver City Board as well as three members of the State Penitentiary Board.

In the meantime, City Hall prepared to resist the Governor's wishes by force of arms. As they prepared for a siege, more than 200 police officers and sheriffs, armed with Winchester rifles and revolvers, barricaded the building. They had plenty of ammunition and a number of sticks of dynamite.

Waite ordered out the First Regiment of Colorado Infantry and the Chaffee Light Artillery. A pair of Gatling guns (an early version of a machine gun) plus two field pieces were brought by 300 soldiers down Lawrence Street on March 14 to City Hall located at Larimer and Fourteenth streets. Nothing like this bizarre scene had ever been witnessed in Denver history, and it brought a crowd of 20,000 spectators, nearly 20 percent of the city's population.

Soapy Smith ordered his criminal element to stand ready to ambush the militia should they move toward City Hall. In a

More than 200 police officers and sheriffs, armed with Winchester rifles and revolvers, barricaded themselves in the Denver City Hall prepared for a siege. (Denver Public Library, Western History Department)

scene more bizarre than any in Denver history, Smith climbed to the building's cupola and held in his hand sticks of dynamite. He dared the militia to fire on him.

Although City Hall was surrounded, Waite wanted a peace-keeping force on hand. He asked the commanding officer at Fort Logan to send in 300 army regulars. They soon arrived at Union Station. Waite also called up all members of the Colorado National Guard and asked that they stand ready at their armories.

To avert an all-out civil war in the streets of Denver, an emergency meeting of the Denver Chamber of Commerce was called. Its members consisted of some of Colorado's most important business leaders, including William N. Byers, David

H. Moffat, Walter S. Cheesman and others. These men convinced Waite to submit the case to the Colorado Supreme Court. On March 17, the case was tendered by Waite's lawyers, and on March 25, it was settled in Waite's favor. However, the high court admonished Waite saying that he had no right to call up the militia to enforce his orders. Jerome C. Smiley, in his 1901 *History of Denver*, wrote of the City Hall war that, "...it was destined to become the most disgraceful affair in the history of the government of our city or in that of the government of any other American city...."

Waite was defeated in the 1894 election, having held office for only two years.

### References

Goodstein, Phil. *The Seamy Side of Denver*. Denver: Denver New Social Publications, 1993, pp. 118 120.

Lamm, Richard D., and Duane A. Smith. *Pioneers & Politicians*. Boulder: Pruett Publishing Company, 1984, pp. 43 48.

Smiley, Jerome C. *History of Denver*. Denver: Old American Publishing Company, (originally published in 1901), pp. 920 927.

# Doomed Monsters

Colorado was known as "The Silver State" since its mines continually increased silver production through the 1880s and into the early 1890s. Prosperity, however, was dependent on the artificial market for silver and gold created by the U.S. government in minting coins of these precious metals. Various laws were enacted, including the Sherman Silver Purchase Act of 1890, to sustain silver production. This act provided for a larger monthly coinage of silver than was the case previously. In 1893, the Sherman Act was repealed and immediately created a depression in the western states known as "The Panic of 1893." The price of silver had been dropping over the years, and the repeal of the Sherman Act was the final blow. Only the richer mines were able to continue operating, and the panic marked the end of an era.

Naturally, the presidential campaign of 1896 was debated, in part, over the silver issue. The Republicans generally opposed the government's further purchase of silver. Most of the Democrats favored its purchase in a ratio of 16 ounces of silver to one ounce of gold. William J. Bryan was the Democratic candidate for president while the Republicans selected William McKinley.

Coloradans were vitally interested in seeing the return of the boom era and the reopening of its silver mines. To that end, a stunt to raise money for the Democratic campaign was staged. It consisted of a head-on collision between two locomotives in an arena near the Union Pacific railroad yards not too far from the Grant smelter in Denver. This idea was not new, and successful collisions had taken place in other states. The collision was to occur promptly at 4 o'clock on the afternoon of September 30, 1896.

Union Pacific locomotive No. 154 became the "Bill McKinley." and No. 153 became the "Mark Hanna." These politicians were against the U.S. government's return to purchasing silver. (Denver Public Library, Western History Department)

A pair of small narrow-gauge locomotives was purchased from the Union Pacific Railroad. They had a 2-6-0 wheel arrangement and were numbered 153 and 154. The engines were in service a dozen years and were virtually identical. One saw service on the Denver, South Park & Pacific and the other on the Colorado Central.

About 10 acres were enclosed with a high fence made of canvas. Through this circular enclosure, a narrow-gauge track was laid on dirt about 1,500 feet in length. An additional 300 yards of track were laid outside the fence on each side of the enclosure. The area was designed to accommodate up to 100,000 people. Promoters expected a crowd of at least 60,000 to show and hoped $2,000 or more would be raised by the event.

It was suggested that one locomotive be named "McKinley" and the other "Bryan." The problem with this strategy was that the wrong engine might get the worst of the collision. One of the engines was named "Mark Hanna." after the chairman of the Republican National Committee. The other was named "Bill McKinley." No matter which engine was destroyed, it represented a Republican.

William H. Jackson captured the crash between two narrow-gauge locomotives in 1896 in an arena just outside Denver. The crash was staged to raise money for Democratic candidates running on a platform that favored the purchase of silver by the U.S. government. (Denver Public Library, Western History Department)

The organizers went one step further than simply naming the engines. Dummies were made to ride in the cabs representing Hanna and McKinley. A dummy of President Grover Cleveland was placed on the pilot of the "Mark Hanna" and a dummy of another Republican sat on the pilot of the "Bill McKinley." The engines were painted red and decorated with bunting and flags. After the decorating was complete, the engines were put on display at Denver's Union Station.

The planned collision velocity was 60 miles per hour. The closest seating to the expected point of impact was 400 feet. The front of the boilers on both locomotives was drilled through, and steam pipes were attached. The steam pipes projected about three feet in front of each engine, much like a lance. They were designed to break off upon impact to allow steam to escape and prevent a boiler explosion.

During the day of September 30th, the two locomotives with their two-car trains were run up and down the track inside the enclosure. The people arrived in the afternoon to witness the collision. They came by street car, train, bicycle, hack, buggy and wagon. Some walked. The sun was warm and the dust awful.

The "Bill McKinley." shown on the right, got the worst of the collision with its tender wedged into the cab. Both locomotives were rebuilt and returned to service. (Denver Public Library, Western History Department)

The affair was advertised extensively to take place promptly at 4 o'clock, and at that hour, there were about 6,000 people inside and many more outside the arena. Every vantage point in the vicinity was covered with spectators. This included the telegraph, telephone and trolley wire poles. Human occupants clung like mammoth birds perched on the very tops of the poles. Every house in the area had people on the roof. Lemonade and soda water vendors were abundant, and every 10th person seemed to be armed with a camera.

Inside the arena people stood around and tried to find places where they could see. In the center of the arena facing the track, an area was roped off and filled with boards laid over railroad ties. These were the so-called reserved seats. A number of lunch stands did a thriving trade while the people waited. At 4 o'clock, the two trains showed signs of life and ran forward, then back through the grounds. The train movements continued at 15-minute intervals for an entire hour.

As the minutes dragged by the crowd began to grow impatient. Nearly all were on time, but they were forced to wait in the heat and dust. This caused much grumbling, especially because the majority had to stand. Finally at 5 o'clock, the engineers and firemen climbed onto their respective locomotives after being given brief instructions. At around 5:15, the trains backed outside the fence. A man with a flag took his place on a chair in the center of the track at the supposed point of impact. The flagman waved his flag. The "Bill McKinley" responded with two short whistles, and the "Mark Hanna" responded from the other side. The flagman waved his flag again, and again the whistles responded. Once more the signal was given with the flag. The "Bill McKinley" started to puff and the "Mark Hanna" did likewise. The engineer on the "Bill McKinley" pulled the throttle wide open, tied down the whistle, and he and his fireman jumped off on opposite sides of the cab as the engine began to move. For some unknown reason, the train of two cars was left behind.

The flagman grabbed his chair and ran away from the track. The crowd noticed that the "Mark Hanna" was doing a vast amount of puffing but was making no headway. The sudden application of power caused the wheels to spin on the track without taking hold. Many of the spectators stood within 10 feet of the south gate where the "Mark Hanna" was to enter. In the meantime, the "Bill McKinley" came thundering and puffing with its whistle shrieking into the arena at an ever-increasing speed. It was now clear that something had gone wrong and that the collision would not take place where it was planned. Soon, the "Bill McKinley" sped past the center of the arena and a warning was given to the people near the south gate to get away quickly. Men, women and children raced back to safety.

The crash took place about 30 feet inside the south gate. The "Mark Hanna" had just begun to pick up speed. The impact was followed by a roar of escaping steam. The estimated speed was only 30 miles per hour, half the speed the promoters advertised. The engines struck squarely and rebounded from the point of impact. The air was filled with fragments of wood and iron, then steam and smoke hid everything. After all the steam had escaped, men and boys climbed all over the wrecked locomotives and picked out small scraps as mementos of the event.

The spectacle was over. The crowd slowly began its way out of the dusty arena back to Denver.

The "Bill McKinley" got the worst of the wreck with its tender torn loose from its frame. The cab was crushed, and one of the pony trucks was driven under the lead driver. The pony truck from the "Mark Hanna" was torn loose and ended up in front of the other locomotive. The "Mark Hanna" had one of its cylinders broken off, and its tender was also torn loose from its frame.

The event did not meet with media approval. The *Rocky Mountain News* reported the next day in its headlines "Fifty cents for a fizz" and "A spectacular disappointment." The *Denver Evening Post* reported, "Badly fooled crowd."

The damaged locomotives were taken to the Union Pacific shops, repaired and renumbered Colorado & Southern 2 and 3. They served the railroad for several more years and were sold sometime prior to 1902.

**References**

Kindig, Richard, E. J. Haley, and M. C. Poor. *Pictorial Supplement to the Denver, South Park & Pacific.* Denver: Rocky Mountain Railroad Club, 1959, pp. 145 156.

The above reference includes the following articles:

*Denver Evening Post.* September 24, 1896

*Denver Evening Post.* September 25, 1896

"Badly fooled crowd." *Denver Evening Post,* September 24, 1896.

"Bumping of the engines." *Rocky Mountain News,* September 25, 1896.

"Fifty cents for a fizz." *Rocky Mountain News,* October 1, 1896.

"Two doomed monsters." *Rocky Mountain News,* September 27, 1896.

"Will come together." *Rocky Mountain News,* September 30, 1896.

# Leadville's Ice Palace

For a brief period of only three months, a great palace stood on the outskirts of Leadville. Its size was stupendous. It covered an area 450 feet by 320 feet, or 3.3 acres. A pair of octagonal towers on the north side of the structure flanked the entrance. These towers had a circumference of 126 feet and stood 90-feet high. The south towers and corner towers were round and measured 60-and 45-feet high, respectively. The palace had the distinctive appearance of a medieval castle. A 19-foot statue on a pedestal graced its entrance. The statue was of "Lady Leadville." and she pointed eastward toward the town's source of riches.

The interior of this great palace was divided into three large rooms and other smaller areas, including an exhibition hall and display rooms. In the center of the structure was a 16,000-square-foot ice-skating rink. To either side of the rink were two 80-foot by 50-foot ballrooms. The east ballroom was designated the Grand Ballroom and was decorated in blue. The floors of both rooms were finished with Texas Pine. The west ballroom was decorated in orange and blue, and its primary use was as a restaurant. The inner walls of each ballroom were glassed in so spectators could watch ice skaters in the comfort of a heated area.

If its size and its location in a mountain valley at 10,000 feet above sea level weren't impressive enough, the primary construction material used to build Leadville's palace was ice!

During 1895, Leadville businessmen started organizing a winter carnival to attract tourists and to put the mining camp "on the map." Originally, it was hoped to have the ice palace ready for the public by Christmas, but unseasonably warm weather almost ruined the partially completed structure. The palace was made of large blocks of ice cut from high-altitude

Leadville's ice palace was located on the outskirts of town. It was construct-ed to attract tourists and to make money for the town. Although a financial failure, it did go down in history as the largest ice structure ever built in North America. (Colorado Historical Society)

lakes in the Leadville area. A Chinook wind in mid-December cut crevices in the ice walls on the shady sides, and the sun soft-ened the south walls. To save the structure, the exterior of the ice palace was sprayed each evening to add frozen material to the walls during the night. The repeated spraying caused the walls to take on a translucent, motherofpearl appearance.

After cold weather returned, the rink was flooded and made ready for skaters. The ceiling over the rink was made of wood and metal trusses. The walls were lined with evenly spaced octagonal ice pillars five feet in diameter that partially hid the wooden supports. Electric lights were frozen into the pillars and walls. Moveable corner lights could be used to illu-minate the frost on the ice-covered ceiling, creating the effect of thousands of sparkling diamonds.

The Leadville ice palace opened January 1, 1896. This marked the beginning of a series of parties, fireworks, outings and general merrymaking in the mining camp. Because of its extremely high altitude, life during the winter months was typ-

The 16,000-square-foot ice-skating rink was in the center of the ice palace. To keep the ice in good condition, it was flooded daily. The ceiling was supported by trusses, and the pillars along the length of the rink partially hid wooden supports within the walls. (Denver Public Library, Western History Department)

ically drab with Leadville residents looking forward to spring. Now the town had its own winter carnival.

The director of the Crystal Carnival Association of Leadville wrote:

> On a massive range,where towering peaks hold white the front of the river's flow,
> We have builded [sic] a house from the Frost King's freaks,
> And invite all the world to play in the snow.

The great, glistening castle of ice gave Leadville a chance to show the world it had "arrived." People could now realize that Leadville was more than a crude, rowdy mining camp.

Leadville readied its hotels, boarding houses and private residences for crowds of visitors to come and enjoy their creation in ice. The railroads offered to put some of their sleeping cars on sidings to accommodate the overflow.

148

To kick off the opening of the carnival, January 4, 1896, was declared "Denver Day." Dignitaries and members of the press were invited to come to Leadville to see the great ice palace. The Crystal Carnival Association met the arriving newsmen at the railroad station and gave them a bucket of red paint to paint the town red and a key to the city.

To attract visitors, the 23-piece Fort Dodge Cowboy Band was hired for the first month of the carnival to play from a balcony overlooking the Grand Ballroom and skating rink. After the first month, local musicians were hired to continue the entertainment.

The ice palace also included a variety of commercial exhibits. Many of these were cleverly frozen into the walls. The breweries were well represented; after all, some of their best customers were Leadville's miners. Zang Brewing, Pabst Brewing, Neif Brothers Brewing and Adolph Coors all had displays. Coors sent six barrels of bottled beer to be frozen into one of the walls of the palace as part of their display. Just in case some of the bottles broke, the brewery sent an extra case of two dozen bottles. The extra case sat around for a while, then turned up missing. A search was made for the stolen brew, and finally after two days, it was discovered in another part of the palace. Out of the entire case, only half a dozen bottles had been opened, which puzzled the carnival officials. Several more bottles were opened, and it was discovered that Coors used salted water colored like beer to prevent the bottles from breaking when they were frozen into the wall. The would-be culprits might have thought the beer went bad and that Coors had lost its ability to properly brew good beer.

Aside from the ice palace itself, there were other attractions in Leadville. Parallel to a couple of the streets were toboggan runs with heated waiting rooms. The starting point for each run was elevated to give riders an extra boost. Young boys were hired to bring the toboggans back for the next group of riders. There were tug-of-war contests, hockey tournaments and curling contests. Local miners from other mining towns participat-

At the entrance to Leadville's ice palace was the statue of "Lady Leadville." She pointed eastward toward the source of the town's riches. The 19-foot statue was sculptured from ice and stood on a 12-foot pedestal.
(Denver Public Library, Western History Department)

ed in rock-drilling contests. The objective was to see which team of two men could drill the deepest hole in a block of granite within 15 minutes. At the depth of slightly over 37 inches, two Leadville brothers won the contest.

The ice-skating rink was the center of attention. It was kept in excellent condition by lightly flooding it with warm water following the afternoon skating session. After three hours, it refroze ready for evening skaters. Prizes were given for the prettiest skater, the fastest skater, the most clever performance, the fanciest tricks and so on.

Leadville's ice palace was designed to make money. Admission was 50 cents for adults, 25 cents for children and a season ticket could be purchased for $25. The entire scheme, however, relied on patronage from Denver. The time required to get from Denver to Leadville over the two narrow-gauge railroads that served the town was more than nine hours one way. Many visitors arrived on a morning train with a sack lunch, paid their admission charge, enjoyed the ice palace and then returned to Denver on the evening train without spending the night. Due to Leadville's remote location, the carnival was a financial failure.By the middle of February 1896, Leadville had grown weary of its winter carnival. The extra police hired to control the anticipated crowds were released. The merchants began to neglect snow removal, and the boardwalks became buried under tons of snow. Attendance by local people dropped sharply.

The Crystal Carnival Association hoped it could operate the ice palace for a full three months, but on March 1, the structure began to melt because of unseasonably warm weather. Nothing could be done to halt its steady decay. On March 28, the ice palace was officially closed. The wind and sun cut the ice away from the wooden framework within its interior, and the great towers began to melt turning the area into a sea of mud. The outbuildings were razed, and the palace's wooden framework stood throughout the summer. In mid-October, the last remnants of the ice palace were pulled down. It was an ignominious end to the largest ice structure ever built in North America.

**References**

Blair, Edward. *Palace of Ice*. Leadville, Colorado: Timberline Books, 1972.

Coquoz, Rene. *King Pleasure Reigned in 1896*. Boulder, Colorado: Johnson Publishing Co., 1969.

Harvey, Mrs. James R. "The Leadville Ice Palace of 1896." *Colorado Magazine*, Vol. XVII, No. 3 (May 1940), pp. 94101.

Weir, Darlene Godat. *Leadville's Ice Palace*. Lakewood, Colorado: Ice Castle Editions, 1994.

Francis Schlatter seemed to have some unique power to heal people. It is estimated that 60,000 or more came to see this man during his two-month stay in Denver. (Denver Public Library, Western History Department)

# The Healer

Francis Schlatter was a man with gentle, child-like simplicity, yet he was powerfully built. This bearded man with long, black hair claimed to be a humble cobbler by trade. In a certain way, he resembled one of the imaginative paintings of Christ.

In the spring of 1895, he appeared in New Mexico looking like a bronze-skinned tramp but with a self-proclaimed ability to heal. Great numbers of people flocked to him just to be touched by his magic hands in the hope that they might be cured. Most came away claiming Schlatter had ended a prolonged illness or restored full function after a crippling disease. Some Coloradans made the long journey south to Schlatter's retreat near Santa Fe to be healed. Eventually, he was persuaded to come to Denver and use his unique power. He arrived in the Queen City in September 1895.

Schlatter was the guest of former Alderman Edward L. Fox. Fox claimed to have been cured of deafness by Schlatter during one of Schlatter's earlier visits to Denver. Schlatter began ministering daily to the multitudes of people who arrived to be healed. They came to Fox's home by the thousands, standing in long lines, waiting to pass by Schlatter to receive his blessing and the gentle pressure of his hand. People also came from the surrounding states. The sick, maimed, deaf, blind and many others were his subjects. Schlatter made no distinction between age, sex or station in life. He refused money or favors and accepted only Fox's hospitality.

As time passed, the daily visitors grew in number until Schlatter was no longer able to touch all who arrived during the course of a day. People began to form a line in the street as early as 3 a.m. and wait until he appeared around 8 a.m. As the chill of winter approached, the multitudes came equipped to

Thousands of people stood in long lines near the home of E. L. Fox in Denver to be healed by Francis Schlatter during the fall of 1896.
(Denver Public Library, Western History Department)

camp and to sleep on the ground, if necessary. During Schlatter's stay, it was estimated that 60,000 or more came to be healed or simply to see this strange man. Thousands claimed to have benefited from his touch. No one questioned the secret of his mysterious power; they accepted him as a healer with God-given power. Many became so devoted that to doubt his power was a sin in their eyes.

Schlatter created a problem for the City of Denver. The healer's fame had spread, and thousands of desperate people flocked to Denver as their last hope. Many only had enough money for the trip, and hundreds could be found wandering the streets. Many applied for financial aid. The health depart-

The Healer

Francis Schlatter
COPYRIGHTED
Nov. 1-95.

In this photograph of Francis Schlatter, his child-like appearance is evident.
(Denver Public Library, Western History Department)

ment visited the Fox residence on November 13, and announced that sanitary conditions were not acceptable. They told Fox that he needed an additional sewer connection to handle the daily crowd.

Schlatter was offered large sums of money to go to other cities, but he refused. He predicted that he would one day disappear and after a time, return again. On the morning following the visit by the health department and about two months after Schlatter arrived, Fox opened the door to Schlatter's room and it was empty. The healer was gone. All of his possessions, except 20,000 unopened letters, also were missing. Fox found a note from Schlatter saying "the Father" had commanded him to leave.

For many days, the disappearance of Schlatter was a matter of great curiosity and a source of grief to those who came to be healed. Fox even resorted to ripping up the boards on his porch where Schlatter had stood and cut them into small cubes that he sold. News arrived that Schlatter was seen riding a white horse into the remote mountains of New Mexico. Other sightings also were made of Schlatter on a horse riding across sandy deserts.

In May 1897, Schlatter's skeleton, saddle, bridle, staff and possessions were discovered in a desolate spot in New Mexico. The unofficial verdict was that he died of starvation. However, in 1909 in a cheap hotel located in Hastings, Nebraska, another man was found dead. The papers found in the room indicated that he was Schlatter. The note he left explained that people would not believe he was Schlatter, and that he was afraid God would take away his power. Just six months later, a 54-year-old man was arrested in Toledo, Ohio, charged with obtaining money under false pretenses. He signed his name as Francis Schlatter, and he claimed to be a healer. After serving his sentence, he disappeared. The mystery has never been solved.

**References**

Cantwell, Larry. "The Healer in Denver." *1971 Brand Book.* Denver: The Denver Westerners, 1972, pp. 163 167.

Hall, Frank. *History of the State of Colorado*, Vol. IV. Chicago: The Blakely Printing Co., 1895, pp. 458459.

Magill, Harry B. *Biography of Francis Schlatter the Healer.* Denver: Schlatter Publishing Co., 1896.

# Central City's Submarine

It is preposterous to believe that Colorado would be the site for the development of a submarine and even harder to believe is that its development was high in the mountains, far removed from any substantial body of water. Nevertheless, on an autumn afternoon in 1898, Rufus T. Owens, of Central City, launched a submarine into Missouri Lake at an elevation of 8,500 feet.

Submarines began to appear during the Civil War, and during the final two decades of the nineteenth century, a number of submarine designs were proposed by a variety of inventors. This activity may have sparked Owens' interest, and in 1896,

Lifted from the bottom of Missouri Lake near Central City in 1944, the Nautilus is raised to the surface. It had been sitting on the bottom of this lake since it was launched in 1898. *The Rocky Mountain News* jokingly termed this the longest dive in history. (Colorado Historical Society)

Owens began his attempt to design such a craft. He was an engineer and was known for his design of the water distribution systems for both Central City and Black Hawk. This same year, the United States was at war with Spain over the sovereignty of Cuba, which was highlighted by the naval battle of Manila Bay. The United States considered submarines to be a potentially effective way of defending its coastline against a potential Spanish invasion.

Owens named his small undersea craft the Nautilus after Jules Verne's fictitious vessel. He hired a pair of Central City contractors to do the actual construction, but he kept the work a secret. Owens' craft, built in a small shed in Central City, was 19-feet long and five-feet tall at its center. It was constructed using a wood frame made of hand-hewn, whipsawed lumber held together by handmade square nails. After completion of the frame, the exterior was covered with irregular-size sheets of iron carefully soldered at the seams to create a seaworthy craft.

On the day of the launch, Owens hired the owner of a local livery company to use a flatbed wagon to haul the Nautilus to Missouri Lake, three miles north of Black Hawk. This was the closest body of water to Central City.

At first, Owens climbed into his craft for its first, untested dive. His friends talked him out of this as being far too dangerous, and he decided, instead, that the craft could be effectively tested using rock ballast. The Nautilus was pushed out into Missouri Lake for her maiden voyage and immediately sank to the bottom.

Possibly out of embarrassment, Owens left Central City within a year, never to be seen again by local residents. He showed no interest in retrieving his Nautilus from the floor of the small lake. Within two years, the U.S. Navy launched its first successful submarine, the Holland.

The existence of the Central City submarine grew more doubtful as time obscured its details. This was combined with the fact that few had actually witnessed the launching, and local newspapers had not recorded the event. During the winter, a

Central City's submarine is housed in a Gilpin County warehouse. The craft lacked any propulsion system or steering mechanism, leading to speculation that the project was nothing more than a whim on the part of its inventor, Rufus T. Owens. (Colorado Historical Society)

surprised ice skater might look down and spot the craft lying on its side a dozen feet below the surface of Missouri Lake.

The Chain O'Mines Company partially drained Missouri Lake during the 1930s, and the Nautilus was completely exposed, thus confirming its existence. Its square hatch was stolen by a souvenir hunter. After the lake was refilled, the public soon forgot about the ship.

During World War II, submarine warfare was in the spotlight, and interest in the Central City submarine was renewed. One of the few witnesses to the construction of the Nautilus, Fred DeMandel, decided to locate and retrieve Owens' ship. As the end of 1943 approached, DeMandel got permission to search the lake by sawing holes in the ice in the general area where the ship was believed to rest. On January 11, 1944, after sawing more than a hundred holes and by using a line with a lead sinker, DeMandel finally found the Nautilus. He confirmed his find using a glass-bottomed bucket to peer into the water.

The foreman of a local trucking company was hired to raise the vessel using a winch. A large hole was cut in the ice above the Nautilus and a steel tripod was erected over the hole. A chain was run through the tripod to the winch. On January 25, the school in Central City was closed along with the courthouse and many businesses to witness the raising of the Nautilus. By the time the submarine was hoisted to the surface, 300 spectators were on hand, and the band from the Central City High School played "Columbia, the Gem of the Ocean."

After the craft dried out, it was put on public display at DeMandel's Central Gold Mine and Museum. It was eventually sold and placed in yet another museum. William C. Russell, Jr., publisher of the *Central City Register-Call* purchased the craft and placed it in a warehouse where it rests today.

Rufus T. Owens built his submarine in secrecy leaving many unanswered questions. The Navy was searching for a practical design at the time, but did Owens intend to submit his design? When the submarine was raised, no propulsion system or steering mechanism could be found. The ballast weighed around 1,500 pounds, somewhat excessive for a first dive. Maybe the entire project was nothing more than a whim.

References

Harper, Frank. "Rufus Owens and his Central City Submarine." *Colorado Heritage*, Autumn 1993, pp. 13 18.

# Colorado's Lightning Lab

A handsome man stood on the rolling prairie. It was night, and the stars penetrated the dark cloak of outer space. The man was dressed in formal attire. He wore a black Prince Albert coat, gloves and a black derby. His thick-soled shoes made him seem tall.

He stood just outside an unusual barn-like structure with walls braced by wooden beams. A flimsy-looking wooden tower rose 80 feet above the ground, and from the tower a metal mast supported a three-foot copper ball more than 200 feet above the ground.

Inside the unusual building were brass bars as big as two-by-fours. In the center of the room was a gigantic cylindrical transformer wound with 40,000 feet of wire. The building was jammed with other equipment, including switches, motors, cables, coils and many other electrical gadgets.

The man in the suit was intent on watching the copper ball high above the ground. He yelled through the open door, "Czito, close the switch." Suddenly, there was a crackling sound followed by a sharp snap. Forks of blue electrical flames began to gyrate around the high sphere, then came a tremendous upsurge of power. A crescendo of loud snaps came from the tower. The noise grew quickly to resemble the staccato from a machine gun. It seemed like the building and all of its strange equipment would explode. The sound continued to build until it reached that of artillery fire and could be heard 15 miles away. The interior of the structure was bathed in blue light from sparks dancing around the transformer. The air became ionized with strange smells, creating the illusion that perhaps the man dressed in black was the devil and had unleashed the furies of hell itself.

Nikola Tesla's laboratory was located just outside Colorado Springs. It was here in 1899 that Tesla created lightning bolts 130 feet long.

(Drawing by Kenneth Jessen)

162

The flames of high voltage electrical energy began to leap from the top of the mast. At first, they were only a few feet long, then, as they grew in length, they became as thick as a man's arm. Eventually, the lightning reached down over 130 feet toward the ground.

Suddenly, the inferno of sparks stopped. The prairie was once again still. The man immediately began to scream at Czito asking him why he had opened the switch and to keep it closed. In the distance, the town of Colorado Springs was plunged into darkness.

The man in the black suit was world-famous inventor, Nikola Tesla, working with his assistant, Kolman Czito. The building was his laboratory where he hoped to perfect a means of transmitting messages through the air from Pikes Peak to Paris. The year was 1899.

Tesla surveyed his laboratory. It was quiet where only moments before he had stood at the apex of his career as an inventor. For a split second he had created man-made lightning using millions of volts, a feat never before accomplished and yet to be repeated.

In the meantime at the Colorado Springs Electric Company's power plant, the night operators were working feverishly to extinguish the fire in their generator. Tesla called the power company asking that his service be restored. The night supervisor flatly refused to provide Tesla with any more electricity for his crazy experiments. Only after pleading with them and offering to completely rebuild the generator did Tesla finally talk the power company into continuing his service.

Some considered Nikola Tesla to be Colorado Springs' mad scientist, but he contributed greatly to the comfort we enjoy today. He invented the most common type of motor used today, the induction motor, and the polyphase system of transmitting electrical energy. Its first practical application was at Telluride, Colorado, where a mine owner transmitted power from a hydroelectric plant to his mine high above the town. This invention became the very foundation of modern power trans-

Nikola Tesla was a handsome man and not afraid to take risks. His high voltage experiments were well known, but his greatest invention was the induction motor. He also invented the polyphase system of transmitting electric energy, which was first tested near Telluride, Colorado.

(Denver Public Library, Western History Department)

mission. The principles used to develop high voltage in a coil are applied today in the automobile ignition coil. Tesla also demonstrated that electrical energy could be transmitted through the air. At the distance of 26 miles from his laboratory, he transmitted enough energy to light 200 incandescent lamps. Tesla was also the first to recognize that radio waves originated from distant objects external to the earth.

In less than a year, Tesla was forced to abandon his work in Colorado. He ran out of money and had to return to New York to work on more practical research. Nevertheless, his Colorado Springs experiments with lightning of his own creation were his most spectacular accomplishments.

## References

Cheney, Margaret. *Tesla    Man Out of Time.* Englewood Cliffs, New Jersey: PrenticeHall, 1981.

Hunt, Inez, and Wanetta W. Draper. *Lightning in His Hand    The Life Story of Nikola Tesla.* Denver: Sage Books, 1964.

Hunt, Inez, and Wanetta W. Draper. *To Colorado's Restless Ghosts.* Denver: Sage Books, 1960, pp. 174 190.

# Quickstep Regains His Job

In 1893, the Denver Tramway abandoned a mile of its trolley line south of Hampton Avenue along South Broadway. M. C. Bogue Jr. purchased a franchise and started a gravity horse car line by purchasing Denver City Railway Car No. 55. The rear platform was reinforced. From Hampton Avenue in Englewood, it was uphill to James Cherry's new subdivision, Cherrelyn. A single horse pulled the car up the grade, and then Bogue led the horse up a ramp onto the rear platform. After a shove, Bogue used the car's hand brake and coasted back to Englewood, all for a nickel a trip. Quickstep was Bogue's first "motive power" for what he named the Cherrelyn Gravity & Bronco Railroad.

It took Quickstep 15 minutes to pull the little four-wheel car up the grade. The trip back required only three minutes, assuming that there were no stops for passengers.

During the summer, the car would stop on a small, wooden trestle over Little Dry Creek to allow a commercial photographer to snap a photo of the horse, car and people hanging out of the windows. On sunny days the horse would sport a straw hat. Passengers enjoyed the ride so much that the horse-powered car remained in service until 1910.

On January 7, 1900, a strong wind began to blow, and materially interfered with the normal operation of the gravity railroad. During the descent, when the car reached a shallow portion of the grade, the wind brought the car to a complete stop. Bogue did not have the heart to ask his horse, Quickstep, to get off and pull. Instead he called upon his passengers to push the car until the grade became steeper.

At the base of the hill on this particular day, Bogue noticed an unusual number of potential passengers waiting to ride.

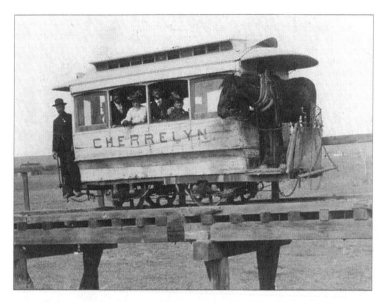

For a nickel a trip, one could ride the Cherrelyn horse-drawn car in Englewood. On the return trip down the hill from Cherrelyn Village, the horse rode on the rear platform. The car is shown crossing Little Dry Creek.
(Denver Public Library, Western History Department)

Also, the velocity of the wind had increased. The situation called for some creative thinking, so Bogue rose to the occasion. For years, Quickstep had been the sole motive power for the car and had hauled it up the hill and had ridden back down countless times. Breaking with tradition, a change was introduced into the locomotion, causing the old horse's importance to dwindle.

Bogue owned other horses, and one of them was pressed into service. The new arrival's duty was to help Quickstep up the hill with the fully loaded car. Where the hill leveled off, the new horse was to wait to help get the car back down the hill against the wind, with Quickstep walking behind to act as a brake if needed.

The innovation worked quite well for the first trip. On the second journey up the hill, disaster struck the entire system, and resulted in a suspension of business for the rest of the day.

**Conductor Bogue is shown with the weathered Cherrelyn horse-drawn car in Englewood. Note the ramp for the horse to get on and off the car.**
(Denver Public Library, Western History Department)

In one place the road ran through a narrow cut, having just enough room for the horses. The sly Quickstep held to the middle of the track and successfully elbowed his new partner up the steep side of the cut. Following was the sound of a heavy fall, and the car came to a sudden stop as it derailed. The people in the car were jarred off their seats and quickly abandoned the vehicle in favor of firm ground.

The new horse had stumbled and fallen. Quickstep, as if in malicious mischief, whinnied and pulled the car over the squirming body of his fallen companion. The new horse was pinned under the front platform, and somehow his two hind legs became tangled in the metal spokes of the car wheels.

It took Bogue nearly two hours to extract the unfortunate horse from his dangerous position. Quickstep pulled the now empty car the rest of the way up to Cherrelyn. As people learned of the accident, they offered advice and sympathy. In response, Bogue delivered a short speech.

Boys, it's my first accident and you bet your life I'll never again use a second horse, no matter how hard the wind blows. Old Quickstep will never have to quit the platform again, either, on the trip back.

References

"Quickstep makes misstep." *Denver Republican*, January 8, 1900.

Robertson, Don, Morris Cafky, and E. J. Haley. *Denver's Street Railways*, Vol. I, 1871 1900. Denver: Sundance Publications Ltd., 1999, pp. 284 288

# Highest Fort in the United States

Extreme situations call for extreme solutions. Fort Peabody was constructed at 13,400 feet in the San Juan Mountains of Southern Colorado to guard Imogene Pass. In 1893, the Western Federation of Miners was organized and began a campaign for better wages, shorter hours and safer working conditions. In 1901, miners in the Telluride mining district won the right to work an eight-hour day. Disputes continued, however, between the union and the mine owners over higher wages. This led to violence, including several murders.

At the reduction mills and cyanide plants in Telluride, about 100 men went on strike September 1, 1903. They wanted their workday reduced from 12 to eight hours to equal that given to the miners. The mill workers also wanted a new wage scale of between $3 and $4 a day. With the mills shut down, there was no place to process the ore, and Telluride's mining industry came to a halt. Soon the union miners joined the mill workers and went on strike.

The mine owners asked Colorado Gov. James H. Peabody to send troops to maintain law and order. The hope of the winnowers was to reopen using non-union workers. Governor Peabody responded by asking President Theodore Roosevelt for 300 U.S. Army regulars. The request was turned down. On November 20, 1903, Governor Peabody dispatched 500 National Guardsmen to Telluride. The men were "flatlanders" from the prairie towns of Lamar and Rocky Ford. The troops arrived November 24, via the Rio Grande Southern Railroad, and set up camp.

It wasn't long before 40 strikers were arrested for vagrancy and "deported" to Ridgway. The rail fare for the 45-mile trip was paid by the county.

Army Maj. Gen. J. C. Bates made an inspection tour of Telluride to report back to President Roosevelt. He concluded, "the disturbances amount to insurrection against the state of Colorado." As more miners were deported, the union president called President Roosevelt, asking for protection for his men. There was no response. Union unrest came to a boil when the mine owners reopened using scab labor. On January 3, 1904, 22 union men were arrested and deported. As the weeks passed, more and more union men were sent out of Telluride.

Telluride officials began to note that some of the deportees were second-time, and even third-time offenders. Guardsmen carefully watched all incoming traffic, including trains and wagons. The only way these union men could be infiltrating was over 13,114-foot Imogene Pass. Mine owners and guardsmen headed up the pass with timbers to erect an enclosed gunner's nest to stop the union miners. The primitive fort was surrounded by a breastwork of rock and was located overlooking the pass.

Troops were posted in this lofty fortification and were under orders to stop and investigate all traffic over the pass. It is a wonder they survived. The fort was located well above timberline and was exposed to high winds. Temperatures, even during the day, might have been well below zero. Although not

Although not an official military installation, Fort Peabody was manned by National Guardsmen during 1904 to prevent union sympathizers from entering Telluride through the "back door" over Imogene Pass. The fort was located at an elevation of about 13,400 feet.

(Denver Public Library, Western History Department)

an official military installation, the fort was named in honor of Governor Peabody. After Telluride was secured, the troops were withdrawn and military control was turned over to a mine manager. He was a former Army captain and had organized the Telluride vigilante committee. His men went on a rampage and forced their way into many homes to rout union sympathizers. Many men were deported. A week later, Governor Peabody was forced to impose martial law, and sent the National Guardsmen back to Telluride. He declared San Miguel County in a state of insurrection.

Using Fort Peabody to keep infiltrators from coming in the back door, Telluride had only to worry about its front door. On April 8, 1904, 74 miners boarded a train at Ridgway for the trip to Telluride. They planned to force their way into town and drive the non-union workers out. The train arrived early in the morning, but the guardsmen had been tipped off, and a heavily armed welcome party, consisting of 100 soldiers and 200 citizens, met the train. The union miners were disarmed, fed lunch and "re-deported" on the next train.

Finally, after 14 months, the mine owners conceded, granting the miners an eight-hour shift and a new wage scale of $3 to $4 per day. Fort Peabody was abandoned, ending an unusual chapter in the unofficial military history of the United States.

**References**

Fetter, Richard L. ,and Suzanne Fetter. *Telluride from Pick to Powder.* Caldwell, Idaho: Caxton Printers Ltd., 1982, pp. 108 117.

Scher, Zeke. "That stormy period when Telluride was in rebellion." *Empire Magazine, Denver Post,* August 9, 1981.

Weber, Rose. *A Quick History of Telluride.* Colorado Springs, Colorado: Little London Press, pp. 35 36.

Jonathan Caldwell's motorcycle-powered aircraft used a flapping motion like a bird rather than a conventional fixed wing and propeller. It was one of several designs for the Gray Goose Airways. (Colorado Historical Society)

# Those Magnificent Flying Machines

Colorado was not without its inventors, especially in the area of flying machines. For example, the *Denver Republican* reported in 1888 that Charles H. Morgan, of Gunnison, invented an "improved" airship using flapping wings for propulsion. The invention was even featured in *Scientific American*.

Morgan's patented airship was listed as light, yet strong. It was roomy and, according to Morgan, could fly easily. He also claimed it was easy to maneuver. Constructed of a series of tubes running the length of the flying machine, the tubes were bent to assume a football shape. The purpose of the tubes was to hold compressed gas, while ribs formed the frame. The patent called for either a metal or silk skin over the frame to act as the airship's cover.

Part of the propulsion system took the form of bird's wings that were used to propel the ship upward and forward as they dipped and stroked through the air. The rudder was the shape of a fish tail and moved back and forth as the machine flew. The compressed gas was Morgan's real secret and was exhausted into chambers inside the ship. Valves were used to control the concentration of the gas and regulate the airship's altitude.

With the flapping, stroking and release of gas, Morgan's airship would have been interesting in flight, but as far as is known, it was never constructed.

Inventor George L. O. Davidson designed a prototype flying machine of enormous proportions. Davidson lived in the Denver suburb of Montclair where he built his aircraft in 1907. This Scotsman claimed he discovered the correct theory for the law of flight. His machine was designed to fly from Chicago to New York City in three hours while carrying 100 passengers.

Morgan's patented airship used structures that looked like bird's wings to propel it forward. The rudder moved back and forth, much like a fish tail.
(Denver Public Library, Western History Department)

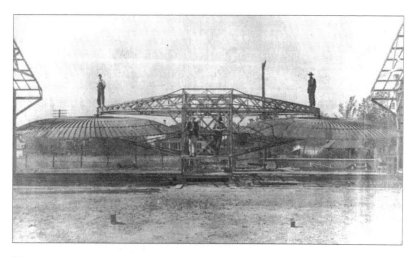

"Gyroscopic rotary lifters" on this machine were supposed to allow it to fly, but its 100-ton weight kept it on the ground.
(Denver Public Library, Western History Department)

"Gyroscopic rotary lifters" made of 110 eight-foot blades were supposed to allow the machine to fly. The lifters revolved horizontally on vertical shafts much like a helicopter. The shafts could be tilted to vary the amount of lift. Rudders fore and aft on the body of the machine were controlled by steering wheels. To power this machine, a pair of 50-horsepower steam engines was used. This was the primary reason why the machine weighed 100 tons. A million dollars was put up to construct a prototype. It is hard to tell what would have happened if Davidson would have had the benefit of modern technology for his project.

A Monte Vista man, William M. Morris, tried for the grand prize of $100,000 at the Louisiana Purchase Fair of 1904 in St. Louis. His new machine, capable of propelling an airship at 100 miles per hour, consisted of a lifting device of some unspecified kind. The machine was to be constructed of lightweight aluminum. Morris claimed his machine could fly upward, forward and backward. Because its inventor feared that someone might steal his idea, he would not give the press any details. Morris asked for $10,000 to perfect his invention, and its details died with him.

Although these inventions did not revolutionize aviation, they represent the creativity of pioneer Coloradans.

**References**
*Colorado Prospector*, Vol. 2, No. 3, (from the *Rocky Mountain News*, June 11, 1903, and *Denver Republican*, January 22, 1888), pp. 3 4.

# Three Governors in One Day

Leave it to Colorado to do something unprecedented in United States history by having three different governors in one single day! The 1904 election was so intense that few Coloradans paid attention to the presidential election contest between Theodore Roosevelt and his challenger, Alton Parker.

The Denver police chief instructed several hundred prostitutes, saloon keepers, ex-convicts and gamblers how to be "repeaters" in the November 1904 election. In exchange, the chief promised "protection" against arrest for their activities. A "repeater" was paid to go from one Denver precinct to another and cast votes along party lines. In this case, it was the Democratic Party with designs to get former Governor Alva Adams re-elected. He was running against the incumbent Republican, James Peabody.

As the Democrats went about planning to stuff the Denver ballot boxes, the Republicans were scheming to steal the election in south-central coal-mining towns with their own strategy of intimidation. Mine owners threatened that if a miner voted for the Democratic candidate, he would be fired. The concept of a secret ballot was thrown out the window. The miners also were threatened with lockouts from their jobs. During the previous administration, the Republicans had conspired with mine owners to squash efforts by the miners to unionize for the purpose of improving working conditions. In summary, the Democrats were a real threat to the stranglehold Republicans held over Colorado miners.

In the meantime on Election Day, the "repeaters" working for the Democrats even resorted to going back to previous polling places in disguises allowing them to continue to stuff the ballot boxes. The day after the election, the police chief

Alva Adams was elected governor of Colorado after the November 1904 election. On March 16, 1905, he was officially ousted from office.
(Kenneth Jessen Collection)

drove the "repeaters" out of town to prevent testimony should the results of the election be challenged.

The end result of the 1904 election was 123,092 votes for Democrat Alva Adams against 113,754 votes for the incumbent Republican Governor Peabody. Peabody immediately protested the election results. A joint session of the state legislature was called to resolve the issue. Chaos erupted throughout Colorado politics, and even the Republicans did not stand united as to who should be governor.

James Peabody was Colorado governor for five minutes on March 16, 1905. He was forced to step down and give the position to Lt. Gov. Jesse McDonald. (Kenneth Jessen Collection)

One telling problem was that several Supreme Court justices needed to be appointed and whoever was elected could slant future judicial decisions in favor of their party. The Republicans agreed to withdraw their protest over the election results only if incumbent Peabody could appoint the new justices before he left office. As a result, Democrat Alva Adams was inaugurated on January 10, 1905. The matter should have ended at this point, but Peabody was clearly a sore loser. He filed yet another protest two days later with the Colorado Secretary of State.

Jesse McDonald was sworn in as Colorado's sixteenth governor on March 16, 1905, after both Alva Adams and James Peabody had held the position earlier in the day. (Kenneth Jessen Collection)

On January 18, Republican Lt. Gov. Jesse McDonald appointed a 27-member committee to decide on who actually won the election. The corruption on both sides could not be hidden as 2,000 witnesses paraded in front of the committee. It resulted in a record 180,000 pages of testimony.

During this process, one particular incident involved Juan Montez, the election clerk for Huerfano County where many of the coal-mining towns were located. The Democrats accused the Republicans of casting a large number of fraudulent votes, and Montez was summoned to appear before the committee. He refused to leave his Walsenburg home until his train fare was paid. He was ordered to bring the ballot box from Precinct No. 23. He failed to comply with the court and was found in contempt. Arrested, he was forced to return to Walsenburg. As the train pulled out of Denver, Montez jumped and hid under the Sixteenth Street viaduct for the night. The police arrested him trying to escape from the Denver area the next day and forced him back on another train bound for his home.

Montez returned with the ballot box, and when it was opened in front of the committee, it found it empty. It did not even contain the required election log. It had not even been used during the election. The officials of the leading coal company, Colorado Fuel & Iron, had decided that Peabody had won the precinct and even dictated the number of votes to be reported to election officials. The *Rocky Mountain News* jumped all over this, stating that this was the most corrupt incident in Colorado history.

It was virtually impossible for the committee to determine who won the 1904 election with its widespread voter fraud. To resolve the issue, a curious scheme was worked out. At 5 p.m. March 16, James Peabody was given the oath of office by Colorado's chief justice, but only after promising to immediately resign. Alva Adams, winner of the election, held the position of Colorado governor during the early part of the day. When Peabody was given the oath of office, Adams was essentially unseated. After five minutes, Peabody resigned leaving the office to Lt. Gov. Jesse McDonald. McDonald was sworn in as Colorado's sixteenth governor. Both Peabody and Adams were bitter over the outcome and made strong statements to the effect that they had been sacrificial lambs by their respective parties.

References

Hornbein, Marjorie. "Three Governors in a Day." *Colorado Magazine,* Vol. XLV, No. 3 (summer 1968), pp. 243 260.

# The Great Horse Race

The *Denver Post* sponsored an endurance horse race in May 1908. First prize was $500, and the distance was 523 miles, beginning at Evanston, Wyoming. The race followed what is now Interstate Highway 80 to Cheyenne, then turned south to its conclusion in Denver. The race was staged to settle the old argument between horse breeders about the durability of the venerable western bronco vs. the eastern thoroughbred.

During the preceding months, the *Post* launched a vigorous advertising campaign to search for entries. Among those who stepped forward were Dode and Ben Wykert of Severance, Colorado. They operated a livery barn and both were good horsemen. They viewed the event as a challenge and purchased a blue roan named Sam from a family west of Ault for $100. The brothers agreed that Dode would ride Sam, and the men began a rigorous training program. The horse was put on a diet of oats with a small amount of hay.

Charles Workman, a resident of Cody, Wyoming, also began training for the endurance race with a horse named Teddy. It was rumored that Teddy was backed by Buffalo Bill Cody and several other wealthy racehorse enthusiasts. Workman rode Teddy 50 miles a day and also rode his horse from Cody to Evanston, a distance of about 500 miles. Teddy looked like such a strong contender that a representative from Cody was sent to Denver with $3,000 for betting purposes.

In all, the race attracted 25 riders; 13 of the horses were full or part thoroughbred. The remaining horses were western broncos. The largest entry was Rose at 1,073 pounds. R. H. Failing, of Littleton, Colorado, was the heaviest rider at 223 pounds, atop a 900-pound chestnut named Tom Campbell. Charles Workman weighed only 160 pounds and was the light-

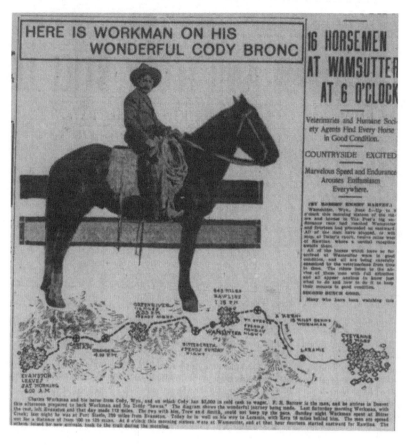

Charles Workman on his horse, Teddy, is shown in the *Denver Post* above a map of the route through Wyoming. (Colorado Historical Society)

est rider. His horse, Teddy, weighed 1,025 pounds.

The *Post* arranged for a special train to transport many of the riders and their mounts to Evanston for the start of the race. The Union Pacific Railroad placed watering stations for the horses along the route. The most difficult section was the Red Desert between Rock Springs and Rawlins. Race rules required horsemen to register, rest and feed their horses every 50 miles.

Early in the morning, May 30, 1908, the great horse race

Dode Wykert and his horse, Sam, are pictured in front of the state Capitol in Denver after completion of their 523-mile horse race that started at Evanston, Wyoming. (Colorado Historical Society)

began with a send-off speech by Wyoming Gov. Marshall Hadsell, followed by a reading of the rules. Amid shouts and shots, the riders took off. Teddy went through three bucking sprees during the early part of the race until he settled down. Workman then put Teddy into a fast pace to outdistance the rest of the field. Wykert and his horse Sam, however, quickly saw how easily they could stay with the leaders.

The first 100 miles across the Red Desert was quite telling

on riders and animals alike. This stretch narrowed the field to 15 riders. Workman and his horse, Teddy, strayed from the course and were forced to backtrack for two hours. They made up the time, and Workman rode Teddy alone into Rawlins at 1:16 p.m. on June 1. They were now 243 miles from the start of the race. W. H. Kern, of Colorado City, Colorado, was only five miles behind. Wykert and his horse, Sam, didn't arrive in Rawlins until the following morning and were dead last.

In the next leg of the race, Workman and his remarkable horse were first into Laramie. When Wykert, riding Sam, entered Laramie, the other riders were well ahead at Tie Siding, Wyoming. Over the Sherman Mountains between Laramie and Cheyenne, Sam showed his real power, and Wykert showed his endurance as a rider. Wykert and Sam pulled into the lead and led the way into Cheyenne 11 minutes ahead of Workman. They were escorted into town by a welcoming committee of 100 riders, including Wyoming's governor.

All the horses were given a thorough checkup in Cheyenne. The field was now down to five, with four of the remaining horses western broncos. All the riders mutually agreed to bed down for the night and start out the following morning at the same time. Workman was given permission by the judges to rest at the stable of one of his backers. Just after midnight, Workman violated his agreement and saddled up Teddy. Quietly they slipped out of Cheyenne under the cover of darkness. One of Workman's backers rode ahead and left a faint trail of flour along the route south to Denver.

Fortunately, a couple of newsboys spotted Workman leaving town and alerted the other riders. Within minutes, Wykert saddled Sam and was off in hot pursuit.

Early in the morning, four of the riders reached Carr, Colorado, and Workman realized his scheme had failed. Wykert's supporters, however, countered with a trick of their own. As Workman slept, Wykert and Sam quietly moved out of sight and waited. Wykert's supporters got a horse and rider of

A very tired-looking Charles Workman, from Cody, Wyoming, is pictured after the conclusion of the great horse race.
(Colorado Historical Society)

about the same size as Wykert and Sam. The rider dressed exactly like Wykert. They left Carr at a terrific pace, and someone shouted to Workman, "Wykert's left! Get the hell out of here!"

Charles Workman leaped to his feet. What he saw were a horse and rider he believed were Sam and Dode Wykert leaving a trail of dust across the prairie. He exclaimed as he rode off, "They won't catch me napping! I'll give them the race of their lives!"

The gap between the horses closed, and as Workman brought Teddy alongside the other rider, he shouted, "Thought you'd fool me, did you?" A reply came back, "Who in the hell would I be trying to fool?"

Workman suddenly realized he had been tricked. He had pushed Teddy hard, and his horse was spent. Wykert was within sight of Workman and could have passed him easily. Wykert, however, showed restraint and saved Sam for the final push into Denver.

Workman arrived in Ault, Colorado, at about 3:45 a.m. A horse named Jaybird was in second place. Wykert jogged Sam in about 15 minutes later. The citizens of Ault built a big bonfire and greeted the riders as they entered town. Wykert caught up with the two leaders by the time he and Sam reached Eaton, Colorado.

Between Eaton and Greeley, Workman's supporters tried another trick. They used an automobile to stir up a cloud of dust ahead of Wykert. The driver kept the car in the middle of the road, blocking Wykert and Sam. Wykert was prepared and pulled out his revolver. When he pointed the gun at the car's occupants, the driver quickly yielded the right-of-way.

In Greeley, all three horses were examined, and Jaybird was ordered out of the race by the veterinarian as unfit to continue. Western broncos Sam and Teddy were now the only surviving equestrian contestants. Teddy was so weak that escort horses were held close to each side to support him. Teddy was given shots to keep him going, and at Fort Lupton, the horse was fed whiskey and quinine. Wykert knew it was just a matter of time and endurance before they would win the great race.

Wykert received a big blow near Brighton, when officials declared the race a draw. Both horses were said to be unfit to go on with their riders, and the riders were ordered to walk their horses the rest of the way into Denver. They were instructed to cross the finish line together. Protests and accusations were shouted at the officials. After all, a lot of money was riding on the outcome.

Using an automobile, the horses were led into Denver along a road lined with thousands of people. As the procession turned on Champa and moved its way toward the finish line in front of the *Denver Post* building, Wykert mounted Sam and made an attempt to pass the pace car. As 25,000 spectators watched, Wykert faked Sam to the left of the car, and the driver maneuvered to block their way. Wykert and Sam then shot ahead on the right to cross the finish line first.

The race had taken seven days, and the horses had traveled 523 blistering miles. Despite the fact that Wykert and Sam crossed the finish line first, the race was still declared a draw. Because Sam was in far better condition, Wykert received the $300 best condition award. Sam lost only 50 pounds during the contest versus 200 pounds for Teddy. Many gifts, including a $500 silver trimmed saddle, pairs of boots, and a riding outfit, were presented to Wykert.

Teddy was unable to move for almost three days, while in contrast, Sam was allowed to graze on the Capitol lawn. Buffalo Bill Cody invited Wykert and Sam to join his Wild West Show on their European tour. Wykert modestly declined the offer.

Wykert said after the race, "...and I will get backing for $5,000 that I can take this Teddy horse over a six-day race and beat him at the finish. I ain't saying that I can stay with him the first few days. No horse can do that and live. But I can come from behind and get him just as I got him this time."

Since only Western broncos finished the race, there was no question that it was far more durable than the thoroughbred.

## References

Black, Winifred. "Man and his bronco!" *Denver Post*, June 1, 1908, p. 1.

Harvey, Robert Emmet. "Workman and Teddy still lead *Post* race."
*Denver Post*, June 2, 1908, p. 1.

Harvey, Robert Emmet. "Workman got start of others." *Denver Post*,
June 5, 1908, p. 1.

Kelly, Elizabeth. "*Denver Post* Race officially decided." *Denver Post*,
June 7, 1908, p. 1.

Krakel, Dean F. "Dode Wykert and the Great Horse Race."
*Colorado Magazine*, Vol. XXX, No. 3 (July 1953), pp. 186193.

Miller, Charles. "Last of the racers has passed Rawlins." *Denver Post*,
June 3, 1908, p. 2.

"Teddy and Sam run dead heat in Great Race." *Denver Post*, June 6, 1908, p. 1.

Van Loan, C. E. "Workman and his big bronco, Teddy, lead race into
Rawlins alone." *Denver Post*, June 1, 1908, p. 1.

Van Loan, C. E. "Four run abreast in lead of *Post*'s Race.." *Denver Post*,
June 3, 1908, p. 1.

Walker, George S. "Endurance race leaders are within a day's ride of the
finish." *Denver Post*, June 4, 1908, p. 1.

Lemuel "Slim" Hecox's head was found buried in an irrigation ditch. He was decapitated by a gang for the large sum of cash he carried in his money belt. (Drawing by Kenneth Jessen)

# His Head at His Side

Paradox Valley is located in the remote southwestern part of Colorado near the Utah border. The only community of any size in the valley is Bedrock. This area lacks the mineral wealth of the San Juan Mountains to the southeast, but there were copper mines in the area. The Cashin Mine operated intermittently during the 1920s, and its owner, Mrs. Gates, employed Lemuel "Slim" Hecox as her trusted watchman. He lived in the small caretaker's cabin next to the mine entrance. Hecox carried his wealth with him in a money belt. It was estimated that around $3,000 to $4,000 was in that belt. He also toted a brace of big .44 caliber six guns for self-protection. Hecox claimed that his name was a misspelling of Hickok and that he was related to the famous gunslinger, Wild Bill. At other times, he said that the money he carried came from the Coffeyville, Kansas, bank robbery.

Although Hecox's stories could hardly pass as the truth, the money was real. His friends advised him time after time not to show off the money belt and to find a good bank to hold his fortune. Hecox's reply was always the same. He would simply pat the handles of his brace of big .44's and practically dare anyone to try to take away his money. To back up his claim, Hecox would display his quick draw and accurate shooting.

During the 1920s, a gang terrorized the Bedrock area. They met secretly in an abandoned building in Bedrock and plotted to drive all law-abiding citizens out of Paradox Valley by using fear and terrorism. They elected to leave an unmistakable trademark of their work. Decapitation of their victims became part of their cult. The head was then buried far removed from the corpse. Because of the large sum of money he carried, Hecox was singled out as the gang's first target.

The younger members of the gang made friends with Hecox. A few days after Thanksgiving 1921, the young men made their way to the Cashin Mine and watchman's cabin. They knocked on the door, and Hecox gladly let them in. Being caretaker at a mine was a mighty lonely life, and he welcomed any visitors. They all sat down at the table in the center of the room, and while they were talking, other members of the gang hid by an open window. When the time was right, one of them fired at Hecox, and the poor watchman died instantly as the bullet passed through his temple lodging in the cabin wall. The gang members then lopped off the dead man's head and took the money belt. They rode up La Sal Creek about 15 miles and buried the head in an irrigation ditch. The headless corpse was dumped in the back of a shack used to store oats for the horses. One bag of oats broke open and spilled on the bloody stump that once supported Hecox's head.

After a few days when the watchman failed to collect his mail, a search was made at the mine. A lot of blood was discovered. The body was found in the shack and placed in a wagon. The wagon was taken to Paradox where some of Hecox's friends began fabricating a coffin. As the body rested in the wagon, some of the oats started to sprout on the bloody stump. As if it could not get more gruesome, chickens gathered around the corpse pecking away at the newly spouted oats.

Hecox was to be buried by his friends, and only the minimum amount of lumber was used to make the coffin. He was laid to rest in the Paradox Cemetery, and his name was carved in a boulder to mark the grave.

One thing the gang hadn't counted on was Mrs. Gates. She hired a trio of the best detectives from Chicago to track down Hecox's killers. After some work and by asking the residents of Bedrock a lot of questions, the detectives learned about the gang's meeting place. A posse was organized and hid near the abandoned building. When the gang arrived, they were arrested.

In this remote part of Colorado, the "law" was not above

Lemuel "Slim" Hecox rests in the Paradox Cemetery with his head tucked under his arm. (Kenneth Jessen)

using a bit of force to achieve desired results. The lonely watchman and his tall tales were dear to the hearts of those who lived in the area. Confessions were quickly extracted from the gang members, and they admitted killing, then decapitating Hecox. They also told where they had buried the head. Montrose County Sheriff Dorsey, with one of the Chicago detectives, had the dubious honor of recovering it from the irrigation ditch.

The citizens of Paradox Valley felt it was only right to bury the head with the rest of his body. Some thought that if they didn't, his restless ghost would haunt the area forever. Hecox's

The store at Bedrock was built around 1876 and is listed on the Colorado State Register of Historic Properties. It is the only historic structure remaining in this town. (Kenneth Jessen)

coffin was dug up and pried open. Since the coffin was only long enough for the headless corpse, and there was simply no room above the shoulders for the missing part. The only choice was to tuck the head under one of his arms.

Slim Hecox's murderers were brought to justice, and as for Slim, he rests in peace in the Paradox cemetery holding his head at his side.

References

Greager, Howard E. *The Hell That Was Paradox*. Self published, 1992, pp. 171 174.

McGaughey, Kathryn. *Below the Rimrocks*. Montrose: Western Reflections Publishing Company, 2003, pp. 63 66.

Rockwell, Wilson. *Uncompahgre Country*. Denver: Sage Books, 1965, pp. 140 144.

# Colorado's Apeman

Sheriff Richards from Fairplay was acting on complaints from local ranchers in the isolated Black Mountain area of South Park. He was told a crazy man was shackled like an animal in a lonely cabin on the 1,200-acre Beeler cattle ranch. Richards and three officers were sent to investigate the rumors on August 20, 1928.

When the law officers arrived, Mrs. Joseph Beeler was sitting on the porch of the ranch house. Her two dogs went into a barking frenzy as the men approached. The officers spotted the log cabin located near the ranch house. They hurried over to the old structure and cautiously peered in through its small window. In the darkness, they could see a human form only by the glistening white of his eyes.

Sheriff Richards realized that the stories of a wild man were true. He pried the padlock off the door, and as the door swung open, the officers stepped into the cabin. The sun hurt the wild man's eyes after a dozen years of living in darkness. His fang-like teeth glittered as Colorado's apeman, Harry Beeler, blinked at the sun. He stared from beneath shaggy, unkempt eyebrows. His matted beard, reaching his abdomen, covered only part of his naked body. A leather belt around his waist was connected to one of the stout chains, and the other end was attached to the cabin wall. A second chain was attached to a leather band around his left ankle. The other end was also attached to the cabin wall.

Harry Beeler sprang at the strangers with a cry like a dog's bark. The chains on the cabin wall stretched tight and abruptly jerked Beeler off his feet. He got up growling and grinding his teeth at the men. The chains prevented him from moving more than three or four feet. In the cabin was a makeshift bed. The floor was piled deep with human waste, and the odor was sick-

**HER FEARS 'APEMAN' WII**

**From Chains to Asylum**

The August 22, 1928, front page of the Denver Post shows Mrs. Joseph Beeler and her insane son, Harry. This was the day Harry was released from his confinement in a cabin on the Beeler Ranch in South Park.
(Denver Public Library, Western History Department)

ening. Insects scurried about in all directions. A tin can on the floor was used for food.

The 70-year-old Mrs. Beeler stood by the cabin and remarked, "He was so bad I couldn't get near him to touch him. He hasn't had a bath in 12 years since we got him back from the insane asylum where they put him after they removed him from the penitentiary. We got him out through Gov. George A.

Mrs. Joseph Beeler kept her insane son chained to the wall of a cabin for a dozen years before he was rescued by local authorities.
(Denver Public Library, Western History Department)

Carlson. I promised to take good care of him. I did the best I could." She continued her story of how Harry didn't even recognize his father. He was so wild that he had to be watched every minute. The only practical thing left for the family was to chain Harry to the wall in the old cabin. Sheriff Richards, upon seeing the tragedy etched on the old woman's face, nodded kindly.

The sheriff and his deputies rushed Harry Beeler from three sides. The insane man fought like a wild animal. Finally, the officers were able to handcuff Beeler, and they threw a blanket over him.

"He hasn't had a stitch of clothes on him for 12 years." Mrs. Beeler related to the officers, "But every night I went out after he went to sleep and threw a blanket over him. Harry is a good boy, Sheriff, and I love him. Harry was a fine looking boy. Any mother would have loved him then in the old days. But who but a mother could love him now as he is today? I don't want them to take him away from me. It would be better if we were both dead. But I don't want Harry to die."

Harry and his aging mother were taken in the sheriff's car to Fairplay. It was the first time in years Mrs. Beeler had been in an automobile. They put Harry in a cell, and Mrs. Beeler was given a room in the New Fairplay Hotel.

News of what the media called an "apeman" spread through Park County. Ranchers and residents came from all over to see Harry Beeler. The sheriff tried his best to protect the Beelers from the public and the media. The next morning, however, people stared through the cell bars at the poor man, and Harry stared back. Then he dashed at the bars like a caged lion. The blanket that Sheriff Richards used to cover him was torn to shreds.

Outside on the main street of Fairplay, Mrs. Beeler protested the way her son was treated. "They won't treat Harry right in the insane asylum." she told whomever listened. "They won't feed him what he likes. They won't cover him at night. They'll just let him die, and while he might be better off dead, I don't want him to die."

Buelah Beeler Evans, Mrs. Beeler's daughter, had died the previous week in a Salida hospital. Evans was known for her books of mounted Colorado wildflowers that sold all over the United States. Since Harry's father, Joseph Beeler, passed away years before, Evan's death left Mrs. Beeler alone to care for her maniac son.

On August 21, 1928, Harry Beeler, age 45, was placed in the insane asylum in Pueblo after a brief sanity hearing in Fairplay. First he was bathed, shaved and clothed. He was then put in a bed in a private room for observation.

Mrs. Beeler lamented, "I'm alone now. I'm going back to the ranch to die. I won't live long and neither will Harry."

The tragic story of Harry Beeler began in 1914 when he was arrested for stealing and butchering a steer belonging to a Cañon City rancher. After bond was Posted, Beeler disappeared. Harry was eventually located in Buffalo, New York, through letters he wrote home. After Harry was brought back to Colorado, he stood trial. The sheriff told reporters he believed Harry Beeler was innocent and had been framed by local ranchers.

Harry, nevertheless, was found guilty and sentenced to a term of two to five years in the penitentiary. After serving a year, Beeler went insane. In 1916, his parents obtained Harry's release to their custody, and this was the last time Harry Beeler was seen for a dozen years. In 1918, Joseph Beeler died in a South Park cattle war leaving Harry's care up to Mrs. Beeler and her daughter.

After Harry's return to the insane asylum in 1928, Mrs. Beeler moved to Pueblo to be close to her son. On May 3, 1934, accompanied by a hospital guard, Harry was escorted to his mother's room in a Pueblo hospital. No light of reason could be seen in his eyes as he looked at the pitiful figure of his mother lying on her death bed. Drawing his head close to her lips, she whispered all her love to him, closed her eyes and passed away.

Harry Beeler died at the age of 60 in 1943 in the insane asylum, bringing to a close the tragic story of Colorado's apeman.

### References

"'Apeman' is calm in insane hospital." *Denver Post*, August 22, 1928, p. 1, 3.

"Authorities scout tale of riches told by apeman's kin." *Denver Post*, August 24, 1928, p. 7.

Bair, Everett. *This Will Be an Empire*. New York: Pageant Press, 1959, pp. 267 281.

Beeler, Mrs. Joseph. "Mother of 'Apeman' tells pitiful story." *Denver Post*, p. 1, 5.

"Blaze razes shack that housed maniac." *Denver Post*, July 29, 1930.

Brady, Ralph. "Chained 'Apeman' rescued from cabin." *Denver Post*, August 21, 1928, p. 1, 5.

"Death of insane survivor ends Beeler cattle king's tragedy." *Denver Post*, August 5, 1943, p. 8.

"Fairplay, 'Apeman' suspected of mystery killing in 1916." *Denver Post*, August 29, 1928, p. 21.

Wayne, Frances. "Mother, loyal throughout life to apeman son, dies in Pueblo." *Denver Post*, May 4, 1934, p. 3.

"Worry over arrest wrecked Beeler's mind, says ex sheriff." *Denver Post*, August 22, 1928, p. 3.

**A Colorado burro named Jenny.** (Kenneth Jessen)

# A Burro Named Prunes

Halfway up Fairplay's main street stands a curious monument made of dull gray cement adorned with ore samples from many of the mines in the Fairplay-Alma area. Etched in the cement is the following expression of respect to one particular burro called Prunes. It reads, "Prunes — a burro — 1867 — 1930. Fairplay, Alma — All Mines In This District." Expressed in this simple inscription is the heartfelt praise to this shaggy little servant of Colorado. Ripley in his "Ripley's Believe-It-Or-Not" syndicated cartoon made Prunes and his monument famous. Prunes also was featured in 1943 on the radio version of "Death Valley Days."

The last mine where Prunes worked was at the Hock Hocking mine in Mosquito Gulch. Prunes became the miners' pet, shuffling back and forth with ore cars in the dark, damp passages. Superintendent Harry Radford maintained that Prunes was his top jackass. When Prunes became too old, his owner Rupe Sherwood freed the jack of his collar and traces, then retired him to roam in the sunlight at will.

When Sherwood was 12, he ran away from home, and after a trip in a covered wagon, ended up hunting with Buffalo Bill Cody. After wandering around the West, Sherwood settled in the Fairplay-Alma mining district. For almost five decades, he owned Prunes and boasted that Prunes worked every mine of any consequence in the district at one time or another.

After Sherwood "pensioned" his faithful jack, the animal spent its final years making the rounds of Alma's back doors begging for food. Residents eagerly gave the old jack food. Flapjacks fried in sowbelly grease made old Prunes hee-haw with delight. As the animal approached his 60s, his health began to fail. An examination of his mouth revealed that Prunes was losing his teeth along with his ability to eat.

A blizzard struck Alma in 1930, and the snow drifted deep. The temperature plunged below zero, and Prunes took refuge in an old shed. During the blizzard, the door blew shut, and a snowdrift prevented the old burro from pushing the door open. Residents noticed that the burro was not making his usual rounds. After searching, they found Prunes half starved in the shed, weak in the legs and unable to walk. He was showered with food and affection, but he did not recover from his exposure to the blizzard.

The miners met in May 1930 in Alma to decide what to do about the suffering animal. It was a difficult decision, and the miners elected to put an end to the suffering of their little long-eared friend. Prunes was shot as some of the old-timers, including Sherwood, wept. His little gray carcass was discarded in a local garbage dump.

A Fairplay cafe owner, with the help of other willing admirers, dug a grave on Fairplay's main street, and here they deposited the remains of Prunes. Over the grave, the miners in the area erected the unique cement monument studded with ore samples from the mines Prunes had worked. Never before had an animal been so honored by a Colorado mining town.

Columnist Arthur Brisbane wrote this about Prunes:

> An old donkey that worked in Colorado mines so long that few could remember when he started is dead at last. He worked until he could not work any more, or even eat. They shot him. Now he is to be honored with a memorial, built of ore samples from all the mines in which he worked. A touching picture, it will be appreciated by many a two-legged worker, including white-collar men...they are less fortunate than the old mine burro. Nobody builds a monument to them and nobody shoots them when they can no longer earn a living. They are turned adrift.

Rupe Sherwood composed a long poem titled "Me and Prunes." which begins:

> So poor old Prunes had cashed in.
>    too bad, still in a way,
> I'm glad the old boy's eased off
>    and calling it a day.
> I'm going to miss him scandalous!
>    The world won't seem the same —
> Not having him a-standin' here
>    hee-hawing in the game.

A year later on August 23, 1931, at the age of 82, Rupe Sherwood died in the Fairplay hospital. On his deathbed, he realized he was on his last trail. He asked to be cremated and have his ashes buried behind the monument under which the

On Fairplay's main street stands this unique monument to a Colorado burro named Prunes. Behind the monument are the ashes of Prunes' last owner, Rupe Sherwood, buried there at his request. (Kenneth Jessen)

bones of his faithful burro were buried. The funeral was attended by about 500 people. A bronze plaque was added to the top of the monument.

### References
Brookshier, Frank *The Burro*. Norman, Oklahoma: University of Oklahoma Press, 1974, pp. 257 259.
Bair, Everett. *This Will Be an Empire*. New York: Pageant Press, 1959, pp. 174 179.
Davidson, Levette Jay. "Rocky Mountain Burro Tales." *1950 Brand Book*, Vol. VI. Denver: The Westerners, pp. 193 203.

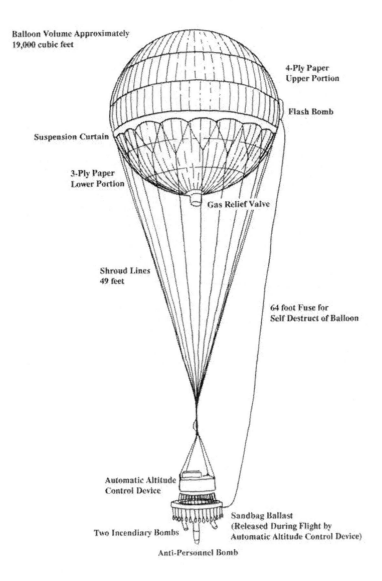

Balloon Volume Approximately
19,000 cubic feet

4-Ply Paper
Upper Portion

Flash Bomb

Suspension Curtain

3-Ply Paper
Lower Portion

Gas Relief Valve

Shroud Lines
49 feet

64 foot Fuse for
Self Destruct of Balloon

Automatic Altitude
Control Device

Two Incendiary Bombs

Sandbag Ballast
(Released During Flight by
Automatic Altitude Control Device)

Anti-Personnel Bomb

The Japanese designated this weapon, the "FU-GO." and it used a balloon constructed of laminated mulberry paper. The Japanese launched 9,300 of these weapons to drift over the United States, using the jet stream to deliver their bombs. (Drawing by Kenneth Jessen)

# Japan Bombs a Colorado Farm

When one first learns that Japan bombed a Colorado farm near Fort Collins during World War II, a picture of a heavily loaded bomber flying low over the Rocky Mountains comes to mind. The bombardier squints through the bomb sight as the aircraft makes its run. But this was impossible with World War II technology, Japanese bombers and the distance involved. Besides, such an event would have been in the history books. The Japanese did, in fact, bomb Colorado, but not using aircraft. A clever scheme of bomb-carrying balloons was part of an offensive to demoralize U.S. citizens. The Japanese released 9,300 of these weapons between November 1944 and April 1945. They counted on the jet stream to carry the balloons over the ocean to the Pacific Northwest where it was hoped the bombs would set fire to our forests.

The balloons were 30 feet in diameter and filled with hydrogen. They carried incendiary and high-explosive bombs along with a timing device. It required 50 to 60 hours to travel over the Pacific Ocean to North America. To compensate for the slow loss of hydrogen, a barometer triggered the release of sandbags during the course of the flight and kept the balloon within its cruising altitude of 30,000 to 38,000 feet. A battery, protected by antifreeze, was used to power the release circuits.

After releasing 32 sandbags during the course of the flight, the altitude control device dropped the load of bombs. This same mechanism also activated slow-burning fuses that set off explosives on both the balloon and altitude control device. This caused the balloon to self-destruct, producing a blinding flash in the sky as 19,000 cubic feet of hydrogen ignited. The capacity of this weapon was limited to 70 pounds and was designed to be unseen until the bombs were released and the balloon exploded. The Japanese hoped to psychologically terrorize the American public using this mysterious, silent device that struck randomly without warning.

The Japanese designated this weapon the "FU-GO" and took almost two years to develop. Denied conventional materials due to wartime demand, the builders turned to the nation's talent for making paper. They used laminated mulberry paper that withstood the cold of the high-altitude flight across the ocean. Balloons were constructed in the homes of civilians, primarily high-school girls, as they pasted the necessary four or five layers of paper together.

The Japanese knew about the jet stream, and the November-to-April launch window was selected since the winds were strongest during this period. The one flaw in their thinking was that during these months, the forests in the Pacific Northwest were the least vulnerable to fires. Snow and rain kept fire danger low.

The launch process depended on good weather and light winds. The balloons were carefully inflated, and it was a dangerous job because of the explosive nature of hydrogen gas. Although they looked under-inflated at launch time, when they reached jet stream altitude, the hydrogen expanded to fill the entire balloon.

Of the 9,300 balloons released, the Japanese counted on a thousand making it across the ocean—enough to inflict sufficient damage on the United States. The Japanese also counted on the media providing detailed coverage of this unusual weapon and panic spreading across the nation due to its mysterious nature.As the months passed after the launch, little news came back to Japan. There was mention in local newspapers of two balloon incidents in Montana and Wyoming in December 1944. Unknown to the Japanese, coverage was suppressed by a nationwide effort involving the cooperation of newspaper editors. Having launched over 9,000 balloons, the Japanese concluded that the FU-GO effort had failed and discontinued further production of the weapon.

A design flaw caused the batteries to fail in the frigid high altitude because the antifreeze solution was too weak. With no power to release the sandbags, the vast majority of balloons descended into the Pacific. Only a little more than 300 reached North America, hardly enough to be effective.

Most of the surviving balloons landed in the targeted area of the Pacific Northwest, however, none of the bombs started major forest fires. Several landed farther downwind in Montana, the Dakotas, Canada, Wyoming and Colorado.There were three confirmed balloon landings in Colorado plus a number of sightings. The most spectacular incident happened on March 19, 1945, near Timnath. At about 2 p.m., a balloon was sighted over Casper, Wyoming, moving to the southeast. By 6 p.m., the balloon appeared over Fort Collins, still traveling southeast. Many residents witnessed the balloon. At 7:12 p.m., a flash came from the weapon followed by a bright ball of fire. Timnath farmer, John Swets, and his 10-year-old son, Bill, were busy working in a shed on some machinery when they heard the explosion. When they went out, they saw a fireball in their newly cultivated field. Sparks flew into the air 10 to 15 feet. A crater measuring about 10 inches in diameter and 46 inches deep was burned into the ground. Black smoke rose from the crater and drifted across the field. By 7:30 p.m., a large number of onlookers from Fort Collins had arrived. After the danger had passed, tail fins were recovered from the remains of a 26-pound incendiary bomb. An unexploded incendiary canister was found near the crater.

A neighbor, Frank Richter, found an unexploded bomb the next day while harrowing his field. It was located a mile and a half from the Swets farm. The weapon was a 10-pound incendiary. A month later, while driving his tractor, John Swets hit a cavern left by yet another bomb—a high-explosive type that apparently exploded underground. No additional bombs were discovered.

The Timnath FU-GO weapon performed the way it was designed, but it drifted well beyond the intended target area.

Because news of the balloon and explosion was suppressed, the Japanese never found out about the Timnath incident during the course of the war.

There were other confirmed balloon-bombs in Colorado near Pagosa Springs, Delta and Collbran. It is likely that other balloons landed in Colorado but were not observed.

### References

Getz, Robert. "The bombing of Timnath." *Choice, Fort Collins Coloradoan,* September 7, 1986.

"Japs bombed Timnath area." *Fort Collins Coloradoan,* August 15, 1945.

Schuessler, Raymond. "Attack on America by Balloon." *Modern Maturity* (FebruaryMarch 1985) p. 4.

Unsworth, Michael E. "Floating Vengeance: The World War II Japanese Balloon Attack on Colorado." *Colorado Heritage* (Autumn 1993) pp. 22 25.

# Elijah, the Marooned Horse

Gordon Warren and Wallace Powell, of Gunnison, were flying over the high Collegiate Range near Buena Vista during the winter of 1956. They spotted a horse trapped on a ridge between Mount Harvard and Mount Yale. Confined to an area about the size of a city block swept clear of snow by high winds, it was obvious to the pilots that the horse would perish unless given some fodder.

Using a Piper Cub, the two Gunnison men began air drops on the 12,800-foot ridge once every few days. Their drops were restricted to times when mountain weather was good. The horse seemed to understand that after the aircraft made an initial pass, it would return to make a drop. Once a bale of hay was delivered, the horse ran over and fed. The mayor of Gunnison, Ben Jorgensen, began paying for the hay and the cost of transportation.

In April 1956, an expedition was put together by the *Denver Post* to reach Elijah and to check on his condition. Because of deep snowdrifts, Elijah could not be brought down from the mountains until later.

(Denver Public Library, Western History Department)

The plight of the marooned horse was brought to the attention of the *Denver Post* by United Airline pilot Ray Schmitt. Schmitt brought in aerial photographs of the animal.George McWilliams, staff writer for the *Post*, named the horse, Elijah, after the biblical character that was fed by ravens when lost in the wilderness. Newspapers all over the world published the story of Elijah and the valiant effort of winged Samaritans to keep the animal alive. Children mailed in their nickels and dimes to continue the air drops. TV crews filmed the stranded animal. Centennial Race Track started a fund for Elijah. Many donations were for $12, the cost of a bale of hay. Airline pilots even pointed out the location of the horse to their passengers. Elijah, the rugged, un-pampered western horse, soon became a national symbol of his four-legged kind.

From a television news report, Bill and Art Turner, of Buena Vista, recognized the horse as one of their pack animals named "Bugs." The Turners recalled that Bugs, a.k.a. Elijah, hated parked cars and women in skirts. He escaped from his mountain pasture the previous fall.The air drops continued. Then in April, a *Denver Post* expedition, including staff writer, George McWilliams; photographer, Dean Conger; copy boy, Irv Moss; the horse's owners; and ski patrol member, Jody Greib, went into the mountains to reach Elijah and check on his condition. It was a long struggle beginning before dawn and lasting until late afternoon, but the *Post* team did reach Elijah. As they came up on the ridge, the Turners called to their animal, and it walked over to them. They placed a rope halter on him and fed him a bag of oats. Elijah was in fine shape. Deep snowdrifts prevented the team from bringing Elijah down at the time.

Later toward the end of May, the Turners climbed through the spring snow and led Elijah down from the mountains. They were forced to shovel a trail through the deep drifts. By the end of the first day, they had made it only part of the way. They tied Elijah to a picket. When the Turners came back the following morning, Elijah had broken his picket rope and was found a mile back toward the saddle.

The people in Buena Vista came out for a homecoming parade to welcome the hermit horse. Elijah was transported to Denver and became the center of attention at the opening of the quarter horse season at Centennial Race Track. He raced another horse named Goliath and won. Elijah was led to the winner's circle and was presented with a red blanket bearing his name in white letters. Elijah was honored with a parade through downtown

rescue Elijah, the snowbound horse.

When Elijah, the marooned horse, was led down from a ridge between Mount Harvard, and Mount Yale, rescuers were forced to shovel a trench through the snowdrifts. (Denver Public Library, Western History Department)

Denver, taken to a carnival at the University of Denver and put on display outside the *Denver Post* building. Elijah was adopted as the official mascot for the Colorado Dude Ranchers Association.

The tale of Elijah was written by Bill Hosokawa, executive news director for the *Denver Post*, and published in *Reader's Digest*. The story appeared in a dozen languages worldwide.

After all the publicity was over, Elijah was returned to his owners to continue his life as a pack animal for hunters and tourists.

During his last years, Elijah was free to roam in his chosen pastures during the winter months, high above the hustle-bustle of humans. In March 1971, Bill Turner came across Elijah, crippled and in poor condition. The 27-year-old horse was suffering from a broken leg and could not be moved from his high mountain pasture. Turner did the humane thing and put a bullet into the indomitable old horse. He didn't notify the media at first because he figured Elijah had already had his share of publicity. Elijah's carcass was left in a cluster of rocks among the tall, majestic peaks. This great Colorado horse lives on, however, in the minds of those he touched.

### References

Fenwick, Red. "Elijah finished his last winter." *Denver Post*, September 19, 1971, p. 49.

Hosokawa, Bill. *Thunder in the Rockies.* New York: William Morrow & Co., 1976, pp. 335 337.

McWilliams, George. "Rescue teams head for Elijah; Humane Society in warning." *Denver Post*, April 12, 1956, p. 2.

McWilliams, George. "*Post* Climbers find Elijah fat and sassy." *Denver Post*, April 13, 1956, p. 2.

McWilliams, George. "Shaggy Elijah rescued from mountain retreat." *Denver Post*, May 24, 1956.

McWilliams, George. "Tale of 'Elijah' snowbound horse circles globe in dozen languages." *Denver Post*, February 7, 1956.

"Of hay in special airlift." *Denver Post*, April 8, 1956.

"*Post* team finds Elijah safe." *Denver Post*, April 13, 1956.

# Curtain Closes the Gap

Sometimes a strange story is a work of art. Bulgarian-born Christo Jaracheff, an artist, was in residence in 1970 at the Aspen Center of Contemporary Art. At this time, he began to survey a site for a curtain to be hung on the west side of the Continental Divide. Already to his credit was the plastic wrapping of a mile of the Australian coastline and the plastic encapsulation of several art museums. He began to survey the area for a curtain and out of 11 potential sites, picked Rifle Gap.

The town of Rifle is a small, western community with a population of just over 2,000. Officials in the town were contacted in January 1971, and they suspected that Christo was some type of escaped lunatic. What Christo proposed was a shimmering orange drapery 1,368-feet long suspended from heavy cables anchored to opposing steep slopes that form Rifle Gap. Town officials knew the curtain was to be done in the name of art, but they thought artists were supposed to paint or create things out of clay, not hang plastic everywhere. With him, however, was Jan Van der Marck, the former director of the Chicago Museum of Contemporary Art. The townspeople began to realize that Christo was serious.The money for the project came largely from European museums as well as from Christo's sale of his drawings and models of cities. The total cost was to be $700,000. To the residents of Rifle, the curtain meant new income from tourists, the press and curtain workers. Also, Rifle was virtually unknown and was not exactly a hotbed of culture. Now with Christo performing one of his famous wrapping-draping works of art, Rifle knew it would become the center of attention.

The custom-made curtain was designed to fit precisely between the craggy slopes of Rifle Gap. It was a technical feat.

This valley curtain was the idea of Bulgarian-born artist Christo Jaracheff. Made from orange, nylon-polyamide fabric, it was strung across Rifle Gap. It remained in place for only 27 hours before the relentless wind through the gap tore it to shreds. (Leo T. Prinster)

Sewn into large, vertical strips, the 200,000 square-foot curtain was fabricated from nine tons of nylon-polyamide fabric. The design and installation required the technical services of a pair of engineering firms plus an industrial contractor. To give the curtain strength against the relentless winds flowing through the gap, it was hung from four steel cables 365 feet above the valley floor. The steel cables were anchored into the slopes by 800 tons of concrete. At the curtain's base was an arched opening 37 feet high and 65 feet wide to allow traffic to flow on the state highway.

After a series of miscalculations, mishaps and delays, August 10, 1972, arrived. It was time to put the curtain up, and what seemed like the entire population of Rifle was on hand to see it. High above, suspended on a steel cable, the furled cur-

This is a proposed work of art by Christo over the Arkansas River between Cañon City and Salida. The fabric would allow sunlight to illuminate the river, and breaks would be made for trees. U.S. Highway 50 can be seen on the left and the tracks of the Union Pacific on the right. (Rendering by Christo)

tain hung. It was then freed from its protective cocoon. Christo was on hand, wearing a white hardhat, to direct the activity much like an orchestra conductor.

The suspense built. A little after 9 a.m., the wind had died. Christo gave the order to unfurl. The orange plastic began to drop by moving down along steel cables. Three-quarters of the way it snagged. "Pull! pull!" admonished Christo. Workers stationed atop the upper cable in a cage prepared to move out along the wire. Just then, a gust of wind pulled the fabric loose, and at 10:35 the curtain was in place.

Like musicians after a concert, the workers were ecstatic at the results. They opened bottles of champagne and threw Christo into the cold water of Rifle Creek.

The curtain was supposed to remain in place for more than a month, but 27 hours later a strong wind carrying sand across the arid area whipped the newly placed curtain into pieces. The untimely demise of his work of art brought no lament from Christo, however. When asked how he felt, he simply stated, "...that the curtain no longer exists only makes it more interesting." When asked why he did things like this, he replied, "For me, esthetics is everything involved in the process — the workers, the politics, the negotiations, the construction difficulty, the dealing with hundreds of people. The whole process becomes an esthetic — that's what I'm interested in, discovering the process. I put myself in dialogue with other people."

In 1995, Christo returned to Colorado to investigate another project. One of the sites was along the Arkansas River between Cañon City and Salida for what he called, "Over the River." The idea was to hang translucent fabric panels above part of a major U.S. river. The panels would be like a canopy and cover the river for up to six miles. The fabric would be suspended by steel cables anchored into opposing sides of the river. The fabric would allow sunlight to illuminate the river, and breaks would be made for trees. The Cache la Poudre River in northern Colorado as well as Idaho's Payette River, and a stretch of the Rio Grande in New Mexico, were also under consideration.

References

Davidson, James Dale. *An Eccentric Guide to the United States*. Berkley, California: Berkley Publishing Co., 1977, pp. 363364.

Foster, Dick. "Landscape artist." *Rocky Mountain News*, July 17, 1995, p. 6A

Glueck, Grace. "The gap that wouldn't stay closed." *New York Times*, August 20, 1972.

# The Tomato Wars

What may have precipitated the Tomato Wars was a comment made to Taylor Adams, former owner of the Inn of the Black Wolf at Twin Lakes along Colorado Highway 82. A woman from Dallas looked at the natural beauty of Twin Lakes nestled next to Colorado's highest peak, Mount Elbert, and said, "This is a pretty area. It's a shame nobody's done anything with it." Taylor knew right then that she had to do something, not about developing the area, but about Texans who constantly try to dominate the economy, roads and resorts.

Many other Coloradans apparently felt the same way. As many as 500 have shown up at the Tomato Wars to plaster the Texans. Taylor, in fact, had a problem recruiting enough Texans to make the war worthwhile. Non-Texans are even pressed into service to help out by momentarily changing their allegiance. It is not desirable to be a Texan during the Tomato Wars. Coloradans historically outnumber them by as much as 10 to one.

To start a war of this sort requires an unusual person with a great deal of imagination. Taylor fits this bill. She is an attractive lady with large brown eyes and short black hair. She probably stands all of 4' 11". Well-educated at Harvard, she was a clinical psychologist. She speaks with a slight hint of a Bostonian accent. Somehow, Taylor managed to escape the hum-drum, work-a-day world for a forested piece of property along Lake Creek that she fondly calls Tapawingo. Anyone who loves the out-of-doors would envy the beautiful view from her kitchen window of the stream with dense forest coming down to the water's edge. Beyond the trees is a rugged mountain rising into the clear, Colorado sky.

The Tomato Wars began in 1982. The contest is held around the middle of September, off season for area resorts. The rules

Taylor Adams, well-educated at Harvard and a former clinical psychologist, started the Tomato Wars in 1982, near Twin Lakes, Colorado. It began as a protest against the Texans who constantly try to dominate the local economy and grew into an annual event. (Joel Radtke)

are simple. Soldiers hit above the torso are considered dead and can return to the bar or watch from the sidelines. The battle against the Texans takes place on Saturday, and on Sunday, there is a shoot-out to determine the overall winner from among all surviving contestants. Incidentally, the Colorado battle cry is, "Keep Colorado beautiful; put a Texan on a bus."

**A mock protester and member of S.P.O.T., the Society for the Preservation of Overripe Tomatoes.** (Joel Radtke)

An army consists of a captain, nine soldiers and an M.P. There is an entrance fee, and for the 1987 war, this was $375 per army. For this particular war, the winning army was awarded a free night at the Inn of the Black Wolf. The fee covers a T-shirt, a party Saturday night with a live band, plenty of beer, a second party Sunday afternoon and plenty of tomatoes. Prizes are awarded for the girl with the best "tomatoes." the Texan with the longest horn and the most imaginative flag. Special prizes are given for the most inventive battle strategy, the best Colorado-Texas joke and the best costume. Mercenaries are encouraged to participate and are assigned to an army short of people.

Colorado bars, and even companies, have sent organized armies to fight the Texans. Creative names such as S.P.O.T. (Society for the Preservation of Overripe Tomatoes), Knights of the Round Tomato and R.I.P. (Rest in Paste) have been used by various groups over the years. Because it is important to identify members of each army in the field of combat, each Colorado army is given a different colored T-shirt. For ease of identification, the Texans wear either white or yellow.

Some of the best strategy has included a Texan arriving by helicopter, a Coloradan arriving by parachute and a peace march held by a dissenting army. In 1984, the inventive Texans moved into battle with a cardboard tank complete with a cannon that squirted tomato juice. The winning strategy one year involved a pretty Texas gal. She began to undress within sight of male Colorado warriors. When the curious Coloradans advanced, they were ambushed from the trees in a hail of tomatoes. A half-dozen casualties resulted before the Coloradans retreated.

During past wars simply to survive, the vastly outnumbered Texans have employed elaborate strategies. They have built forts of plastic garbage bags and straw bales and dubbed the forts "the Tomalamo." The Texans located their forts on the south side of Lake Creek, and the flag from the Lone Star State was used to mark its location. The Tomalamo typically has been the scene of the most intense fighting. Incidentally, Lake Creek is temporarily renamed the Rio Grande for the sake of the Tomato Wars.

Adams "conditions" the ammunition by letting it freeze and thaw for several nights. This has a marked softening effect. During the more recent years, five tons were used, divided into 265 cases. Each army is typically given three to four cases, and some of the more successful armies are able to steal several more cases.

**Serious fighting at one of the bunkers during the 1989 Tomato Wars near Twin Lakes. Note the ammunition boxes.** (Joel Radtke)

To review a typical war, a bugle sounds at noon, and the throwing begins. As the Coloradans charge across the "Rio Grande." tomato missiles hit the water all around them much like depth charges. In response to an all-out assault by the Coloradans, the Texans usually retreat quickly to their fort. They defend their fort by throwing tomatoes at a rapid pace. During some of the battles, the Colorado armies run out of ammunition and are forced back across the Rio Grande. Ultimately, however, the numerically superior Coloradans surround the Tomalamo, "kill" all the Texans and bring down the Lone Star flag. This process usually takes about two hours. The hillsides are left running red with tomato juice and, the ground becomes littered with shreds of tomato skins that look like they came out of a blender.

According to Adams, the Texans refer to their ammunition as "to-MA-ters." while the more sophisticated Coloradans often use the term "tom-AH-toes."

During the heat of battle, tomatoes fly in all directions and are split into pieces by tree branches. The soldiers carry their ammunition in plastic grocery sacks strapped to their waist. Many of the participants come dressed in strange outfits and even blackened faces. Some are intoxicated, which seems to aid in combat or lessen the agony of defeat. To be drunk, by the way, is technically against the rules. At times, there are close-range encounters between two people faced off only feet apart, throwing tomatoes at one another at a machine-gun-like pace. Bobbing and weaving seems mandatory to stay in the game.

The strategy of some warriors is to simply hide in the woods until the Texans are defeated and the armies are fighting among themselves. These warriors then come out of hiding and wipe out the remaining troops. The survivors on Saturday come to the finals the following day. The first year, the winner was determined by a game of musical chairs where one chair held an overripe tomato on its seat. During the following years, duels were fought at 20 yards. Finalists were not allowed to move their feet and throwing continued until one of the two combatants got plastered.

Some years, protestors showed up dressed in outrageous costumes carrying signs, "Hell no, we won't throw," and spouted slogans that tomatoes should be used for Bloody Marys, salsa, barbecue sauce and other uses. The mock protestors chanted, "Make paste, not waste."

Dressed in a Cuban-style general's outfit, a warrior known only as General Gambola showed up at the 1986 war. He had cartridge belts containing Havana cigars. A female warrior dressed in a sheepskin outfit with a painted face held a shield high with the words "Tomato Warrior" painted on it. Maybe the best flag that year was from an army called "Gypsum's Finest" from Eagle, Colorado. It showed an eagle dropping tomato bombs on an armadillo.

The battle zone has varied over the years. For the 1982 and 1983 encounters, the war zone was in a field south of the Inn of the Black Wolf. In 1984 and 1985, the war zone was moved to the upper end of the lake, and from 1986 on, the Tomato Wars were held on Taylor Adam's property along Lake Creek.

### References

Carrier, Jim. "Seeing red." *Denver Post*, September 27, 1987, p. 6B.

Frazier, Deborah. "Splat! State ripe with pride after smearing Texas in Tomato War." *Rocky Mountain News*, September 27, 1987, p. 34.

Personal Interview with Taylor Adams on September 3, 1988, at her home near Twin Lakes, Colorado.

Personal Interview with John Slater on September 3, 1988, at the Nordic Inn, Twin Lakes, Colorado.

Jameson, Betsy. "Colorado Tomatoes Puree Texas Invaders." *Network* (December 1984), pp. 1619.

Knox, Don. "5th Tomato War makes'em see red." *Rocky Mountain News*, September 14, 1986, p. 40.

McCoy, Joan. "Twin Lake Inn is rustic, friendly." *Rocky Mountain News*, March 6, 1983, p. 50N.

McCarthy, Larry. "Tomato Wars." *Philip Morris Magazine* (Spring 1988), pp. 34 37.

Noriyuki, Duane. "Tomato War party swings at Twin Lakes." *Rocky Mountain News*, September 30, 1984, p. 8.

"Twin Lakes gears up for annual Colorado vs. Texas Tomato War." *Loveland Reporter Herald*, September 13/14, 1986.

# Eqilogue

## *Unusual Events*

Coloradans continue to be imaginative, if not a little strange, as illustrated by some of the state's contemporary events. Take for example Guffey resident Bill Soux who hatched the idea of the "Chicken Fly" in 1986. Young chickens are rented for $5, then forced out of a mailbox with a toilet plunger from a 12-foot tower. The distance the bird flutters is measured, and within every flight of 10 birds, a handmade prize is awarded to the person with the chicken that flies the farthest. It's the kind of event where grown men wait in line, holding their chickens and stroking their feathers, and joking about being hen-pecked.

Once ejected, the confused fowl flies or flutters to the base of the tower. The record distance is 138 feet, and many birds fly more than 60 feet with some landing in the audience. A tape measure, tied to the base of the tower, is used to measure the distance. Children, selected for their quickness, are employed as chicken chasers to recover the freed birds.

United Poultry Concerns, however, cried "foul" to this event. These activists tried to stop the "Chicken Fly." saying that it causes fear in the bird and teaches cruelty to animals. Even if the bird is not physically harmed, say the poultry activists, it teaches that it is fun to overpower defenseless animals into doing things that are not natural. It should be noted that no bird has ever been physically injured in the Chicken Fly. Psychological damage is unknown.

Turning to a cold story, Bredo Morstøl was born near Romsdel, Norway, in 1900, and spent his career as the head of the parks for that region. He died of a heart attack in his sleep in 1989. In anticipation of finding a way to revive him using future

A flying fowl at the Guffey's annual Chicken Fly provides Fourth of July entertainment for this Park County town. (Kenneth Jessen)

technology, he was cryogenically frozen. His relatives shipped his body to Oakland, California. In the meantime, his grandson, Trygve Bauge, constructed a cryogenic laboratory in an unlikely location—Nederland, Colorado. Grandpa Morstøl was moved to Nederland in 1993 and packed in dry ice. After Bauge was deported for an expired visa, keeping a frozen corpse in town met with stiff opposition from town officials. Such activity was banned, however Grandpa Morstøl was grandfathered in. Bauge continues to pay the bill to bring 1,500 to 1,800 pounds of dry ice to Nederland once a month. Although dry ice fails to meet cryogenic standards as applied to suspended animation, it at least keeps Grandpa from smelling.

Things are pretty slow in Nederland in March, and "Frozen Dead Guy Days" was created to celebrate Grandpa Morstøl. It has attracted sponsors like North Face (makers of warm ski apparel) and Tuff Shed (the brand of shed that houses

**Coffin races are the highlight of "Frozen Dead Guy Days" to celebrate Nederland's famous cadaver, Grandpa Morstøl.** (Kenneth Jessen)

Grandpa). Naturally, the general theme is the cold and the dead. The U.S. Post Office even got into the act with a special cancellation stamp for letters mailed during the event. The parade down Nederland's main street features coffins followed by hearses. Coffin races are the highlight of the weekend, but there is also a Grandpa look-alike contest, a rib-eating contest and the brain freeze. For $25, one can tour the Tuff Shed where Nederland's most famous corpse is stored.

The coffin races are held on a snow-covered course to make the footing tricky. Each team of five uses four members as pallbearers and carry the fifth member as a live corpse in the coffin around the course. A mandatory stop is made at the town playground, the corpse leaps out, races up a slide, slides down and then hops back into the coffin. The pallbearers carry the coffin the remaining distance around the course that includes a rather steep bridge. The team with the best time wins.

Leadville's "Boom Days" celebrated in August has an outhouse race. It is the sequence of the events that is of interest. The burro race for men is the first event of the day followed by the women's burro race. While lined up on Harrison Avenue, the trusty little animals sense that they are about to be prodded and forced to run over the highest through-road in North America at 13,188 feet. This gives them a natural urge to lighten their load. With little or no street sanitation, a gunfight follows. The next event is "the mosey." with families dressed in nineteenth-century costumes, including ladies in long, flowing dresses that drag along in what the burros discarded.

Despite tricky footing, the outhouse races follow. To provide a level playing field, the same outhouse is used by each team in this timed event. The outhouse is equipped with castors, and to make it "street legal." it sports a Colorado license plate. One member rides while the others pull and push the little building down the street. Impressive times are achieved.

Other outhouse events include the Friends of the Walden Library annual barns and outhouse tour that raises all of the money for the library's book budget. Attendees pay $10 to be taken around

Dressed to the nines, Kris and Rex Shaw stand in front of one of their highly decorated outhouses in Walden during the annual barns and outhouse tour. (Kenneth Jessen)

225

Impressive times are achieved at Leadville's outhouse race despite tricky footing, thanks to what the burros left on Harrison Avenue. This is part of the town's annual "Boom Days" in August. *(Sonje Jessen)*

North Park, where at each stop the history of that particular ranch or structure is given. Included in the fee is a barbecue held at the end of the day complete with live music.

California's Hobart Brown originated the idea for the "Kinetic Sculpture Challenge" covering 38 miles in three days. Rich Hartner brought a version of this event to Boulder in 1980, and it has been held annually ever since. It caught on immediately with 60 teams entering the first year with an estimated 25,000 spectators. The race was originally run across 14 miles of farmland, ditches, dirt roads and water between Niwot and the edge of Boulder. To prevent ecological damage and traffic jams, the event was moved to the Boulder Reservoir and shortened to 4.6 miles in 1982.

Held in May, it is a race over land, through mud and across the surface of the Boulder Reservoir. The variety of human-powered conveyances has been practically limitless and so have the costumes worn by the racers. David Rahn, organizer of this event for many years, notes that it is really not a race and that finishing first place is only a minor part in the scoring. This is reflected in the awards handed out, including Free Spirit, Commodore Cup, Best of 10 and High Visibility Award.

The Kinetic Sculpture Challenge is more about style, costumes, theme, creativity and perseverance. Each team selects a theme, such as Lizard of Oz, Mutants on the Bounty or Poultry in Motion. Engineers, mechanics and welders build a human-powered machine, while other team members sew and stitch costumes.

On September 10, 1945, Lloyd Olson's wife asked him to kill a chicken for dinner. The chicken, Mike, survived for 18 months without its head. This has led to Fruita's "Headless Chicken Days" in May. Manitou Springs rings in the New Year with a fruitcake toss. Crested Butte celebrates "Flauschink" in the latter part of March with the festival's king and queen carrying toilet plungers as their scepters.

Certainly, some of the events held in Colorado are not in good taste and may not be politically correct. They are creative and are generally in good fun.

## Destructive Rampages

On the darker side of bizarre behavior have been several notable rampages. For example, in February 1998, Thomas Leask took an earth-moving piece of equipment and ripped apart several of Alma's buildings, including the town hall. He also shot to death the town's former mayor. Leask was sentenced to life plus 27 years.

As far as destruction, 52-year-old Marvin Heemeyer tops them all. He secretly used the equipment in his muffler shop to convert a Komatsu D355-A bulldozer into an armored tank. To prevent exposure to police gunfire, he steered his homemade tank using seven closed circuit TV cameras. On the dashboard, he could switch the monitor between cameras. An oxygen tank, with piping to each camera lens, was used to blow away debris in front of the lens. Inside were three ammunition boxes. One supplied a .223-caliber Ruger Mini-14, another for a .308-caliber Fabrique rifle and the third for a .50-caliber Barrett 82A1 semi-automatic rifle. Each gun had its own gun port. Every vulnerable part of the bulldozer's machinery was covered with armor. Concrete was sandwiched between two layers of heavy steel plate, making rounds from a high-power rifle ineffective.

On June 4, 2004, Heemeyer attacked Granby businesses damaging or completely destroying 13. The 410-horsepower machine simply was unstoppable. As Heemeyer's tank ran through the Gambles store, it fell through the floor. It was stuck unable to go forward or backward. Heemeyer took a .357-caliber magnum revolver and shot himself. It took hours for the police to get inside the tank and remove his body. His vendetta against Granby originated over long-brewing feuds he had with the city and certain business owners. Part of the dispute was over recent zoning laws. To ensure that he would complete his mission, police found a hand-written list of businesses in the bulldozer's cab that Heemeyer planned to attack.

## Colorado Mayors

Former Shotgun Willie's stripper, Koleen Kae Brooks, was elected to the office of Georgetown mayor. After many stormy days in office, according to the *Rocky Mountain News*, she flashed her ample breasts in a Georgetown bar. She then claimed that she had been assaulted. To this, police charged Brooks with filing a false police report. Ousted by a recall election, she temporarily hosted a radio show on Denver's KBPI.

Georgetown has some of best-preserved Victorian homes in Colorado. It is also the location of the historic Hamill House. Certainly Brooks added color to the town, but tarnished its dignified reputation and angered many residents. However, not all is a loss. Much to the disgust of many, tourists visit her tanning saloon to be photographed with Georgetown's famous ex-mayor.

In Guffey, the town provides some refreshing insight on how a well-oiled political machine should operate. Although shy at first, it is possible for a stranger to spend quality time with the town's mayor. The mayor often greets visitors, even in the rain. The mayor's office is on a tattered sofa in the dark interior of the Guffey Garage, one of the town's antique shops. Curled up in front of a potbelly stove, Guffey's mayor has a disarming way about him and visits are always pleasant.

Guffey's mayor, Monster, relaxing at home. (Kenneth Jessen)

For those not versed in Colorado politics, the mayor is a friendly, black cat named Monster. Park County officials wanted some sort of central government in this outpost, and its 35 residents first elected a golden retriever. In a succeeding election, Monster became mayor. Discounting the fact that three of its citizens were shot to death in 2001, Guffey appears to be politically more advanced than many other Colorado mountain towns.

## Unusual Buildings

There are many strange structures in Colorado. Located along the Greenhorn Highway (Colorado 165) southwest of Pueblo is probably Colorado's most unique building, Bishop Castle. It was constructed by one man, Jim Bishop. It must be experienced to appreciate its size and complexity. Made from rubblestone and held together with concrete and steel, it is more of a work of art than a building. One tower rises 160 feet above its surroundings. The castle has an external staircase extending up one of the flying buttresses to a large room. For those afraid of heights, there is an irregular spiral staircase in the interior. In keeping with his philosophy, Bishop asks nothing to see or enter the structure. He wants it open to rich and poor alike. However, there is a donation box and gift shop where souvenirs can be purchased.

He wrote a booklet called *Castle Building* that he autographs, "Jim Bishop (Castle Builder)." The booklet is less about castle building and more about fighting the bureaucracy of the U.S. Forest Service, the Colorado Department of Transportation and, most recently, Custer County officials.

It is a work in progress, and Bishop occasionally will use an old truck to hoist more mortar and rock up to the top using a pulley system. He works alone at heights near 200 feet on rickety scaffolding without the benefit of any safety equipment.

In 1963, architect and inventor Charles Deaton started work on a home located on the side of Genesee Mountain west of Denver. He called it the Sculptured House, but it looked more like a flying saucer that had landed in the trees. The house did not have any vertical walls. The floor on the lowest level was curved like a dish. Deaton ran out of money, and the house remained unfinished.

In 1973, Woody Allen used the house for a film titled "Sleeper." From that point on, it has been known as the Sleeper House.

Larry Polhill purchased the property and blasted away a flat area so that a more practical living addition could be con-

Bishop Castle, located southwest of Pueblo, is more of a work of art than a building. Thousands have visited this structure, Colorado's most unique building. (Kenneth Jessen)

structed. Again, the house remained unfinished. John Higgins in 1999 bought the place and poured over a million dollars into tripling its size and making it livable. When Higgins first toured the property, every window had been broken by vandals and a fox was living in one level. Now this home has over 7,000 square feet of living space with five bedrooms, five bathrooms, a four-car garage and many other features.

**References**

Adato, Allison. "A Most Unusual Race." *Life*, Vol. 19, No. 8 (July 1996), pp. 24 25.

Aguilar, John. "Armored dozer was bad to go." *Rocky Mountain News*, June 25, 2004, p. 34A.

Brennan, Charlie. "Bankruptcy, recall taint Brooks' year." *Rocky Mountain News*, January 4, 2003.

Brennan, Charlie. "Fingernails chip away at defense." *Rocky Mountain News*, January 8, 2003, p. 6A.

Espinoza, Annette. "Dead Guy Days alive, kicking." *Denver Post*, March 14, 2004, p. 1B.

Florio, Gwen, and Julie Poppen. "Granby faces rebuilding job." *Rocky Mountain News*, June 5, 2004, p. 8A.

Frazier, Deborah. "Mayor collars popularity." *Rocky Mountain News*, July 21, 1997, P. 8A.

Gonzalez, Erika. "Tuff sell." *Rocky Mountain News*, March 12, 2004, p. 6D.

"Guffey a gem in the rough." *Colorado Springs Gazette*, December 3, 1993.

"Kinetic sculptures sail Saturday." *Denver Post*, May 5, 1989.

McCullen, Kevin. "Boulder's kinetic contraptions to tackle mud, lake and land." *Rocky Mountain News*, May 5, 1989, p. 14W.

Mehle, Michael. "Floating their boats in kinetics race, winning is beside the point." *Rocky Mountain News*, April 30, 2004.

Meyer, Jeremy. "Poultry activists oppose Guffey's chicken fly event." July 4, 2003, *Colorado Springs Gazette*, p. 5.

Montero, David and Owen S. Good, "Rage fueled man's assault on Granby." *Rocky Mountain News*, June 7, 2004, p. 1A.

Poppen, Julie. "Nederland's icy escapades." *Rocky Mountain News*, March 15, 2004.

Rebchook, John. "Asking $10 Million in round figures." *Rocky Mountain News*, September 3, 2003, p. 1B.

# About the Author

**Author Ken Jessen**

Kenneth Jessen is best known as author of *Ghost Towns, Colorado Style*, a three-volume set covering more than 600 town histories. His most recent work is *Out the Back, Down the Path – Colorado Outhouses*. Other books include *Railroads of Northern Colorado, Thompson Valley Tales, Eccentric Colorado, Colorado Gunsmoke, Bizarre Colorado, Estes Park – A Quick History, Georgetown – A Quick History, The Wyoming Colorado Railroad* and *An Ear in His Pocket*.

In addition to books, Jessen is the author of more than 850 articles plus several booklets. His column on Colorado ghost towns and regional history has been a weekly feature in the Sunday edition of the *Loveland Reporter-Herald*. He is a contributor to *Lydia's Style Magazine, North Forty News, Colorado Time-Table* and *Colorado Central Magazine*. Jessen has made a half dozen appearances on "Colorado GetAways" (KCNC – Channel 4) and presently serves as an adviser. Jessen had a monthly radio show on Clear Channel KCOL 600AM. In addition to these activities, Jessen is a tour guide for the Colorado Historical Society and the Estes Park Museum. He also gives lectures on area history.

A life member of the Colorado Railroad Museum, Jessen is a longtime member of the Rocky Mountain Railroad Club, a Centennial member of the Colorado Historical Society and one of the founders of the Western Outlaw-Lawman History

Association. He is also a patron of the San Luis Valley Historical Society. Other memberships include the Estes Park Area Historical Museum, the Johnstown Historical Society, Summit Historical Society, Loveland Historical Society, Fort Collins Historical Society and the Westerners. Jessen has served as a volunteer for Larimer County Parks and Open Space and completed nine years on the Loveland Public Library Advisory Board. He presently serves on the Cultural Services Board for the City of Loveland.

On April 13, 1883 in the Lake City courthouse, cannibal Alferd Packer was tried for the murder of his five companions. It was the first trial of its type held in Colorado. (Kenneth Jessen)

# INDEX

*Italicized indicates illustration*

| | |
|---|---|
| Adams, "Captain" Samuel | 27, *28* |
| Adams, General Charles | 45 |
| Adams, Gov. Alva1 | 76, *177* |
| Adams, Taylor | 215, *216* |
| Adolph Coors | 149 |
| Allen, Woody | 230 |
| Alma | 199, 227 |
| Anthony, James | 96 |
| Arnold, Philip | 37 |
| Ashbaugh, Eldon | *86* |
| | |
| Baggs, "Doc" | 33 |
| Bailey, Doc | 22 |
| Balaam | *59* |
| Barnum, Phineas Taylor | 68 |
| Bates, Maj. Gen. J. C. | 169 |
| Bean, Luther | 108 |
| Bedrock | 189, *192* |
| Beeler, Harry | 193 |
| Beeler, Mrs. Joseph | 193, *195* |
| Bell, Wilson | 47 |
| Bishop Castle | *231* |
| Bishop, Jim | 230 |
| Black Hawk | 7 |
| Boggs, Professor John L. | 71 |
| Bogue Jr., M.C. | 165 |
| Bonfils, Frederick G. | 3 |
| Boulder | 226 |
| Breckenridge | 27, *31* |
| Brisbane, Arthur | 200 |
| Brooks, Koleen Kae | 228 |
| Brown, Hobard | 226 |
| Brown's Park | 39, 101 |
| Bryan, William J. | 140 |
| Byers, William N. | 18, *138* |
| | |
| Carson, Gov. George A. | 90, 194 |
| Carson, Kit | 19 |
| Cash, Mrs. Charles | 52 |

| | |
|---|---|
| Cashin Mine | 189 |
| Central City | 157 |
| Central Pacific | 38 |
| Cherrelyn horse drawn car | *166, 167* |
| Chicken Fl | 223 |
| Cody, Buffalo Bill | 125, 187 |
| Colorow, Chief | 21 |
| Conant, William A. | 67 |
| Conger, Dean | 208 |
| Cook, Charles A. | 25 |
| Cornwall | 10 |
| Cozens, "Uncle" Billy | 7, *8* |
| Creede | 110 |
| Croffut, George | 79 |
| Crystal Carnival Association | 148 |
| Czito, Kolman | 163 |
| | |
| Davidson, George L. O. | 173 |
| Davis, Carlyle C. | 77 |
| Deaton, Charles | 230 |
| DeMandel, Fred | 160 |
| Denver City Hall | *138* |
| Denver, South Park & Pacific | 87, 119 |
| Diamond Peak | *43* |
| Dorsey, Sheriff | 187 |
| | |
| Elijah | *207, 209* |
| | |
| Fairplay | 193, 198, *201* |
| Fitzsimmons, Bob | 116 |
| Fort Peabody | 168, *170* |
| Fox, Alderman Edward L. | 153 |
| Fruita | 227 |
| FU GO | *202,* 203 |
| | |
| Gardner, Charles "Big Phil" | 17 |
| Gardner, Cotter, Brewer and King | *36* |
| Garfield, President James A. | 81 |
| Genesee Mountain | 230 |
| Gerry, Judge Melville B. | 50, *53* |
| Gilbert, Paul | 2 |

# INDEX

| | | | |
|---|---|---|---|
| Gonzalez, Francis | 105 | Inn of the Black Wolf | 217 |
| Gordon, James A. | 17 | | |
| Granby | 228 | Japan | 203 |
| Great Sand Dunes | *108, 109* | Jaracheff, Christo | 211 |
| Griffin Monument | *122* | Jessen, Kenneth | 233 |
| Griffin, Clifford | 121 | Jonathan Caldwell's aircraft | *172* |
| Guffey | 222, 229 | Kehler, Jack | 7 |
| Hadsell, Gov. Marshall | 183 | Kinetic Sculpture Challenge | 226 |
| Hafen, LeRoy | 4 | King, Clarence | 38 |
| Harney, Gen. William S. | 17 | "knockers" | 15 |
| *Harpers Weekly* | 48 | | |
| Hecox, Lemuel "Slim" | 189 | La Caverna del Oro | 1 |
| Heemeyer, Marvin | 227 | Leadville | 65, 142, 146 |
| Higgins, John | 232 | Leadville Ice Palace | *147, 148, 150* |
| Horn, Elisha P. | 2 | Leask, Thomas | 227 |
| Hosokawa, Bill | 125, 209 | Los Pinos Agency | 46 |
| | | Lynch, Pat | *100*, 101 |
| Imogene Pass | 169 | | |

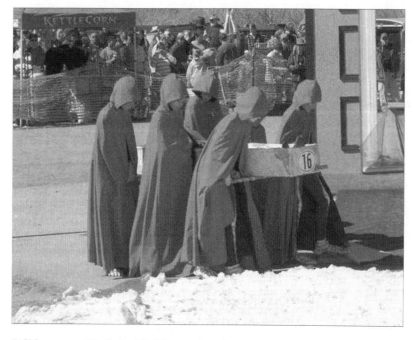

**Pall bearers at Nederland's "Frozen Dead Guy Days" held in March of each year.** (Kenneth Jessen)

The idea for Guffey's annual Chicken Fly was hatched by resident Bill Soux in 1986. This is the launch tower. (Kenneth Jessen)

| | | | |
|---|---|---|---|
| Marble Mountain | 1 | Montgomery | 21, 22 |
| Maud, Lady | 126 | Montrose Placer | |
| McDonald, Gov. Jesse | 179 | Mining Company | 131 |
| McKinley, William | 140 | Morgan, Charles H. | 173 |
| McWilliams, George | 208 | Morgan's airship | 174 |
| Missouri Lake | 158 | Morris, William M. | 175 |
| Monster | 229 | Morstøl, Bredo | 222 |
| Montez, Juan | 179 | Mount Silver Heels | 21 |

# INDEX

National Guard 169
Nederland 223
Noon, George 47

Ogilvy, Lyulph Stanley *124*, 125, *128*
Ohio Creek 87
O'Keeffe, Sergeant
John Timoth 57
Old Mose 91
Ouray, Chief 45
Over the River *213*
Owens, Rufus T. 157

Packer, Alferd 45, *47*
Paradox Cemeter 190, *191*
Parris, Lloyd E.5
Peabody, Gov.
James H. 168, 176, *178*
Perkins, James 98
Pigg, Wharton 93
Powell, John Wesley 101
Powell, Wallace 206

Radliff, Jacob 91
Redford, Harry 199
Rickards, Sherif 193
Rifle 211
Ripley's Believe It Or Not 198
Rollins Pass 26
Rollins, John Q. *24*, 25
Rollinsville 26
Russell, William C. 160

San Francisco 37
Sangre de Cristo Mountains 1, 104
Schlatter, Francis *152*, 153, *155*
Schmitt, Ray 207
Shaw, Kris and Rex *225*
Shelburne, E. 68
Sherman Silver

Purchase Act 135, 140
Sherwood, Rup 199
Signal Service 56
Silverthorn, Judge Marshall 29
Slack, John 37
Sleeper 230
Smith, Jefferson Randolf "Soapy"
*112*, 113, *114*, *117*, 135
Solid Muldoon 69
Soux, Bill 222
Spangler, Michael 34
Spanish Cave (see La Caverna del Oro)
St. James Methodist Church 12
Starr, Professor James 54
Stein, Orth 77
Swets, John 205

Tammen, Harry 129
Tesla, Nikola 163, *164*
The Great Rock Wall *86, 88*
Tiffany and Company 38
Tippett, Bishop Donald H. 14
Tomato Wars 215
Turner, Bill 208
Turner, Col. N. P. 131
Union Pacific 38, 141
Uzzell, Parson Tom 115

Valley Curtain *212*
Vance Junction *85*
Vance, Colone 184

Waite, Gov. Davis H. 135, *136*
Warren, Gordon 206
Western Federation of Miners 168
Windsor Hotel 125
Workman, Charles 181, *182*, *185*
Wykert, Ben 181
Wykert, Dode 181, *183*

Yoeman, J.H. 2

Zang Brewing 149

**238**